GETTING *the*
**PRETTY**
BACK

itbooks

AN IMPRINT OF HARPERCOLLINS*PUBLISHERS*

# GETTING *the*
# PRETTY
# BACK

### FRIENDSHIP, FAMILY, AND
### FINDING THE PERFECT LIPSTICK

*Molly Ringwald*

ILLUSTRATIONS BY RUBEN TOLEDO

A hardcover edition of this book was published in 2010 by It Books, an imprint of HarperCollins Publishers.

GETTING THE PRETTY BACK. Copyright © 2010 by Ringwald, Inc. All rights reserved. Printed in China. No part of this book may be used or reproduced in any manner whatsoever without written permission except in the case of brief quotations embodied in critical articles and reviews. For information address HarperCollins Publishers, 10 East 53rd Street, New York, NY 10022.

HarperCollins books may be purchased for educational, business, or sales promotional use. For information please write: Special Markets Department, HarperCollins Publishers, 10 East 53rd Street, New York, NY 10022.

FIRST IT BOOKS PAPERBACK EDITION PUBLISHED 2011.

*Designed by Lorie Pagnozzi*

Library of Congress Cataloging-in-Publication Data is available upon request.

ISBN 978-0-06-180945-3 (pbk.)

13  14  15  16  SCP  10  9  8  7  6  5  4

THIS BOOK
IS DEDICATED TO PANIO,

**AND TO ALL WOMEN.**
OUR MOTHERS AND
OUR DAUGHTERS

CONTENTS

GETTING *the*
PRETTY
BACK

# INTRODUCTION

# HOW I LEARNED TO **STOP WORRYING** AND LOVE THE **F-WORD**

IT HAPPENS TO ALL OF US. Here is how it happened to me.

On February 18, 2008, I turned forty years old. It hardly seemed possible. I felt like I was just out of my teen years—a sentiment that in my case happens to be shared by a lot of people. The enormous popularity of the films I made as a teenager has succeeded in essentially freezing me in time for the general public. In the minds of most viewers, I will always be sitting on a table eating birthday cake with a hunky senior.

Like most women, I was sort of dreading the day. Unlike most women, I didn't have the luxury of fibbing about my age, or even being

I

coy when asked. Even my poor mother has experienced the fallout when she was paying a bill recently and the waitress innocently inquired if she was Molly Ringwald's grandmother. And while it is nice in some way to be seen as "youthful," the fact remains that I am no longer a teenager, and no amount of reruns on cable is going to change that.

For months leading up to my birthday (let's just call it B-Day) I had well-meaning friends call and e-mail my husband incessantly about what kind of special plans we had in mind. He kept them at bay by saying he would let them know. Then he would gently nudge me, saying that I could do whatever I wanted—a big blowout party to end all parties, or a simple dinner at home together. He just wanted to know what I wanted.

"Let me think," I would moan. "I'll decide tomorrow . . ."

Eventually he stopped asking, and I don't know what he told my friends. Finally, the day before B-Day, I did some soul-searching. What did I really want for my fortieth birthday? A yoga retreat? An overnight flight to Miami? Botox? Then, as if from the ether, a voice spoke with astounding clarity.

*Fondue.*

Of course. If I had to turn forty, I would celebrate it by eating cheese. And not just any old cheese, but the yummiest, most decadent, melt-in-your-mouth kind of cheese—made only more decadent by the warm crusty bread that you dunked into it. So, in the dead of winter, ten of my closest friends and I bundled up in our layers and traipsed over to Artisanal, a famous cheese and wine bar in New York City, and ordered bowls of fondue. I made sure I wore a red dress under my winter coat, drank delicious red wine, ate amazing gooey French cheese, and laughed with my friends until I was forty years old and one day.

Here's a secret: I actually like my age. Or rather, I like everything that I've learned as those years have been accumulated. Whether it has to do with friendship, family, or falling in love, whether it involves acting, fashion, or motherhood, there's nothing that I would give up. (Well, OK, maybe I'd pass on the Dorothy Hamill haircut I got in the fourth grade.)

This book is about celebrating turning forty and being the sexiest, funniest, smartest, best-dressed, and most confident woman that you can be. It's about everything I've learned, thus far, and how to put it together and incorporate it all. It doesn't matter if you're married, divorced, remarried, or eternally single . . . the one thing we have in common is that we *all* turn forty and wonder how we got there—and what we're going to do now.

· · · · · · · ·

Two months after my fortieth birthday, I was asked to be a part of a show about teenagers. There was that word again! *Teenager.* It seems to stick to me like a barnacle. But the difference was that now I was not being asked to *play* a teenager, but to play the *mother* of one. Once I got over the shock (I was still recovering from the fact that I had just turned forty. And for those of you who have gone through it, you know what I'm talking about. For those of you who have it still coming—it gets way better, I promise) I realized that the show was a great way to bring it all full circle. Surrounded by teenagers and their urgent high school dramas, I felt a mixture of nostalgia and relief. Nostalgia at seeing my younger self reflected in them, and relief that I was no longer agonizing about things like popularity and acceptance in the same way.

When you're a teenager, you're forever thinking: *Do they like me?* When you're a grown-up, as anyone over the age of thirty can attest, the question becomes: *Do I like them?*

Happily, the show has been a great success, and I am constantly looking for ways to portray a "cool" mom—a mom that all of those characters I played way back when would have liked to have had. At the same time, it gives me a chance to think about the kind of mother I want to be for my own children, and what kind of woman I want to be . . . for myself.

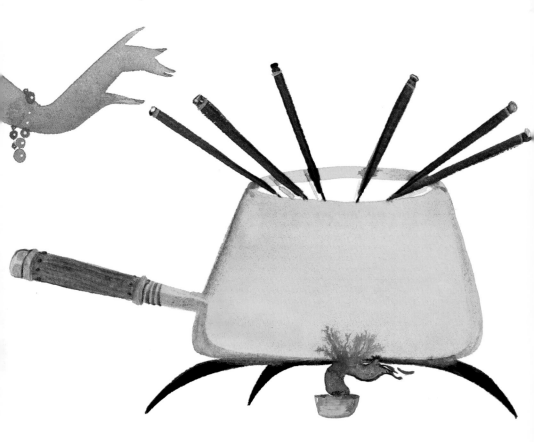

# ARTISANAL BLEND FONDUE

*serves 6*

Kosher salt

1 clove garlic, end cut off
and discarded

3 cups shredded Comte,
Emmenthaler, and Vacherin
cheese (for 12 ounces total),
at room temperature

1 tablespoon plus 2 teaspoons
cornstarch

1 cup dry white wine

1 teaspoon freshly squeezed
lemon juice

1 pinch nutmeg

Black pepper in a mill

1. Put 1 teaspoon salt in a fondue pot or a heavy-bottomed, 2-quart stainless-steel saucepan. Vigorously rub the exposed end of the garlic over the surface of the pot, starting in the salt and coating the entire surface. Discard the garlic.

2. In a medium bowl, combine the grated cheese and cornstarch, mixing well to distribute the cornstarch evenly. Set aside.

3. Add the wine and lemon juice to the prepared fondue pot and bring to a boil over medium-high heat.

4. Once the liquid has come to a boil, slowly add the cheese and cornstarch mixture, whisking continuously. Make sure each addition is completely melted and incorporated before the next addition.

5. Once all of the cheese has been added, cook it over medium heat for one minute. Season with nutmeg, salt, and 4 grinds of pepper, or to taste. Remove the pot from the heat and serve.

EMBELLISHMENTS: *Serve the Artisanal Blend Fondue with cubed bread. Day-old bread is best, but any crusty bread will work well. The Artisanal Blend Fondue may also be served with boiled fingerling potatoes, sautéed beef tips, pickled vegetables, or air-dried beef, kielbasa, and/or sausage.*

Chapter One

# ISN'T IT PRETTY TO THINK SO

EARLY ON DURING MY FIRST PREGNANCY, A FEMALE ACQUAINTANCE OF MINE TOLD ME, "YOU BETTER HOPE SHE ISN'T A GIRL, 'CAUSE SHE'LL SUCK THE PRETTY OUT OF YOU!"

I sort of laughed. Sort of.

In a few short weeks, I found out that the baby was a girl. A few weeks after that, I was absolutely sure that the woman was right.

· · · · · · · · ·

I was not a particularly attractive pregnant person. Every woman I know has wanted to be "beautifully pregnant": the type of cover-girl pregnant where you can't tell from behind—it's only until you turn and reveal the perfect bump hovering above your Manolos that you are *with child*. Me? I blew up like a water balloon (thanks to a semicommon ailment, preeclampsia . . . and a troubling, powerful fondness for "macho nachos"). The freckles on my face decided to band together and form a pigment block party, and my ankles swelled as if I'd been stung by a hive of particularly vindictive bees. On the day my daughter Mathilda was born, as I tried to tie up loose ends before heading into the labor room, I was asked to participate in a maternity Gap ad—which I was obviously unable to do. When I hung up the phone and told my husband and friend Victoria, the nurse on call chimed in, "That's funny! A Gap ad? You look like the Michelin Man!"

My husband, friend, and I were shocked into silence. The nurse took this to mean that we hadn't heard her and felt compelled to repeat her insight.

"You look like the Michelin Man!" she snorted.

It wasn't till she went in for the third time that Victoria snapped, "Yeah, we *got* it."

. . . . . . . . .

In the months after I delivered Mathilda, I would catch glimpses of myself in the mirror, each time thinking the same thing: *Is that me?* I couldn't get over the heft of my body. I would breast-feed my daughter and look down in horror to find that my breasts were larger than her head.

My husband came home from work one day to discover me in the bedroom, dissolved in tears.

"It's true! It's true . . ."

"What's true?" he asked, alarmed.

"She got it all. She sucked the pretty out of me . . ."

I'm sure I'm not the only woman who has felt this way, and obviously it isn't only motherhood that can give you this feeling. It can be a relationship gone south, a stressful job, weight gain. What makes it so disturbing when it is motherhood, however, is the completely irrational feeling that your loss is someone else's gain. Something that is so associated with something so wonderful. The giving of life. It's the ultimate bittersweet sensation.

It seems to me that there is a moment when women are no longer defined as "pretty." It's hard to know when exactly it happens, but suddenly you notice it. You are "beautiful," "unique," "handsome" (if you're unlucky), or "interesting." *Pretty* is a word that is reserved for the young. At some point you are expected to relinquish the word like an Olympic torch. If you were ever called pretty to begin with, you know that there is a definite time limit imposed on

> MANNERS ARE ESPECIALLY THE NEED OF THE PLAIN. THE PRETTY CAN GET AWAY WITH ANYTHING.
> —EVELYN WAUGH

the word. You could say that it has the longevity of the career of an ice-skater or ballerina. You get to dance *Swan Lake* a few times, then you're expected to teach it.

What is pretty anyway? Not just beauty. It's an attitude toward life, a frame of mind. A lightness, even a frivolousness. It's attractive and charming—yet also naïve. It's endearing, particularly because it is so innocent, because it seems to disregard (or simply be unaware of) all the things in the world—the experiences, the people, the accidents—that increasingly defy and deny this sense of giddy hopefulness.

When I told a friend I was writing a book called *Getting the Pretty Back*, she asked, "Why don't you call it *Getting the Beauty Back*? That's a better title." But beauty isn't what I'm talking about. Prettiness is inside every woman; it's a feeling, a sense of self that never entirely leaves. It's always there. I remember at my daughter's baptism, which we had in Greece (where my husband's parents live), watching my mother-in-law dancing at the after party at four in the morning. As she spun I could see the village girl she had been fifty years earlier in every light, joyful step. It was moving and it was inspiring, and it was also—the best part— completely, carelessly normal. She wasn't thinking about it.

PUT YOUR HAND ON A HOT STOVE FOR A MINUTE, AND IT SEEMS LIKE AN HOUR. SIT WITH A PRETTY GIRL FOR AN HOUR, AND IT SEEMS LIKE A MINUTE. THAT'S RELATIVITY.

—ALBERT EINSTEIN

She wasn't pretending. She was just doing what felt right. I watched her turning her wrists and hands in time with the music with such confidence and grace, thinking to myself, *She's so pretty.*

Getting the pretty back is about getting back in touch with your essential self: the part of you that knows what you really want, that takes risks, that isn't scared away by all the things that can—and have—gone wrong. It's the part of you that runs around in summer holding your sandals in your hand. It's remembering the girl you were at fifteen who did double flips off the high dive, the girl who laughed and squealed with your best friend while you huddled together in the bathroom, double piercing your ear with a needle and a potato.

· · · · · · · ·

Being pretty can be about style or outer beauty, true, but on a deeper, more fundamental level, it's about learning to take care of yourself again. Style is the first and easiest step to reminding yourself—and the world—that you matter. Too often, after kids, after years in and out of relationships, we settle. We stop paying attention to ourselves. Everyone else's needs come first. We'd love to try a yoga class or see a movie with a friend or visit a country that we have never been to, but before that can happen, we have all these other responsibilities. The car payments, the mortgage, the dental appointments, the carpools, the birthday parties, the work functions . . . at times, they can make you feel as if adulthood is nothing more than a series of tasks to be completed.

And I'm not advocating trying to recapture your youth—mostly because it is impossible, but secondly, because you shouldn't want to. Our life experience, after all, is what makes us interesting, smarter, more confident, and formidable. But being all those things shouldn't preclude being whimsical, light, flirty, and fun. At heart, prettiness is a state of mind. It's a way of looking at things, of looking at ourselves. It's just one thread of the tapestry that makes us up, but it's an important, all-too-often neglected thread.

Luckily, it isn't so hard to get the pretty back—as I rediscovered again while writing this book. I spent a lot of time searching through my past—remembering the good and bad and finding out what got me to where I am now. I invite you to do the same. Whether it's reconnecting with friends that you miss, or remembering how much you used to love to dance to Bananarama in the living room by yourself, getting back in touch with the pretty girl that you once were might just make you realize that she really isn't so far from the woman you are today.

*Drink, pretty creature, drink!*

—WILLIAM WORDSWORTH

IT CAN HARDLY BE A COINCIDENCE THAT NO
LANGUAGE ON EARTH HAS EVER PRODUCED THE
EXPRESSION "AS PRETTY AS AN AIRPORT."

—DOUGLAS ADAMS,
*THE LONG DARK TEA-TIME OF THE SOUL*

# THAT'S THE THING ABOUT GIRLS. EVERY TIME THEY DO SOMETHING PRETTY, EVEN IF THEY'RE NOT MUCH TO LOOK AT, OR EVEN IF THEY'RE SORT OF STUPID, YOU FALL HALF IN LOVE WITH THEM, AND THEN YOU NEVER KNOW WHERE YOU ARE.

—J. D. SALINGER, *THE CATCHER IN THE RYE*

HARK! HARK! THE LARK AT HEAVEN'S GATE SINGS,
/AND PHOEBUS 'GINS ARISE,/HIS STEEDS TO
WATER AT THOSE SPRINGS/ON CHALICED FLOWERS
THAT LIES;/AND WINKING MARY-BUDS BEGIN/TO
OPE THEIR GOLDEN EYES:/WITH EVERY THING THAT
PRETTY IS,/MY LADY SWEET, ARISE,/ARISE, ARISE!

—WILLIAM SHAKESPEARE, *CYMBELINE*

MY DEAR YOUNG LADY, THERE WAS A GREAT DEAL
OF TRUTH, I DARE SAY, IN WHAT YOU SAID, AND
YOU LOOKED VERY PRETTY WHILE YOU SAID IT,
WHICH IS MUCH MORE IMPORTANT.

—OSCAR WILDE, *A WOMAN OF NO IMPORTANCE*

TO LOOK ALMOST PRETTY
IS AN ACQUISITION
OF HIGHER DELIGHT
TO A GIRL WHO HAS
BEEN LOOKING PLAIN THE
FIRST FIFTEEN YEARS
OF HER LIFE THAT
A BEAUTY FROM HER
CRADLE CAN EVER
RECEIVE.

—JANE AUSTEN, *NORTHANGER ABBEY*

HE REMEMBERED THAT SHE WAS PRETTY, AND,
MORE, THAT SHE HAD A SPECIAL GRACE IN THE
INTIMACY OF LIFE. SHE HAD THE SECRET OF
INDIVIDUALITY WHICH EXCITES—AND ESCAPES.

—JOSEPH CONRAD, *VICTORY*

Chapter Two

# IT WOMAN

WHEN I WAS SEVEN YEARS OLD, I WAS A TALL LEGGY KID WITH SHORT SHAGGY HAIR AND PERMANENTLY STUBBED TOES, AND FOR A GOOD DEAL OF TIME I SPORTED A WOMAN'S STOCKING (MY MOTHER'S) ATTACHED TO THE TOP OF MY HEAD WITH TWO PRE-CISELY CRISSCROSSED BOBBY PINS. This seemed to be, in my seven-year-old brain, the best solution as to how to exist in California in the seventies with a gorgeous blue-eyed older sister with long blond hair. I was sure that she knew how it tortured me as I lay on the bed and watched her brush her long straight tresses, and then flip it back over to have it land on her back, as if in slow motion. I was mesmer-ized by the perfection of it. It was the perfect color, the perfect weight. It even smelled nice. (Farrah Fawcett Shampoo, which I'm pretty sure was just Herbal Essences with a picture of Farrah stuck on the bottle.) I asked my mother if I could grow my hair out like my sister's.

"Maybe later," she'd tell me. "This time we'll cut it short, then you'll see. It'll grow in *thicker!*" This lie, handed down from the ages, clearly senseless and yet somehow, at that age, irrefutable. And anyway, who doesn't want thicker hair? So off to the barber I'd go, where they'd chop off my honey-colored wisps and fashion my hair into a boy's cut.

"A pixie," my mom would say.

"What's his name?" everyone else would say.

In our neighborhood, in every direction out of our cul-de-sac, there was a home that housed a set of siblings: Joanie and Jennifer to the left of us; Lorie and Lisa to the right; and Karen and Krista in the middle, across the street. (Not one of which, incidentally, had anything short of shoulder-length hair.) Our games mostly consisted of freeze tag and cartoon tag, and I occasionally could corral them into taking part in a backyard vaudeville show. I had copied out scenes from classic Abbott and Costello sketches from a local show that my brother and sister and I performed in on the weekends. I would direct them into the proper timing and sometimes have to explain the joke. "Yeah, you see his *name* is Who . . . and see, the other guy doesn't get it!" This would keep us occupied until the ice cream truck or another distraction came along. And then home for dinner.

Then one day while playing inside the house, rummaging through my mother's things, I came across a long ponytail curled up in a hatbox that I was pretty sure wasn't real, but nevertheless intrigued me almost as though it were a living, breathing thing. Treating it with reverence, I carefully presented it to my mother for explanation. (I don't even think that it matched my mother's hair color.)

"Oh, it's a *fall*," she said. "We used to wear those all the time a few years ago. Nobody wears them anymore."

This information I accepted gladly, since it basically gave me free rein to claim the thing as my own. I would attach it to my head, and no one would be able to pry it loose. Unfortunately, there was precious little to attach it to. Every time I thought I had it fixed, the second I attempted to copy my sister's hair swing (that I'm sure she copied from Susan Dey), the flick from one shoulder to the other, the hairpiece would fly off my head and sail across the room. (Apparently this unhappy event actually happened to a famous singer/dancer on Johnny Carson's *The Tonight Show*, which my mother remembers helped to deter her from wearing the elaborate updo. "And they were really going out of style anyway . . .") This did little to deter *me* until I had to face the fact that as much as I loved this piece of hair and wanted it attached to me, the thing had no interest in me, preferring to hibernate indefinitely in the hatbox.

I reasoned that the real problem was the weight of the hairpiece, and if I could just find a less weighty version . . . unfortunately, my mother had not invested much in her hair accoutrements. There were only two that I could find, and one of them I figured was a Halloween wig and of little interest, since it was a short curly do that looked like it belonged to *Bewitched*'s Samantha's frisky cousin Serena. But I did happen upon a pair of stockings—one for each leg. While panty hose were becoming more commonplace, my mother still owned the old-fashioned singular nylons, which along with the "fall," I never saw her wear. The thought occurred to me that it was about the same length as the fall and a much better color match. Two bobbies later, I was in business. I flicked my head around and admired my handiwork. Then I ventured out into the neighborhood.

My friends made no mention of my new hairdo. If they even noticed, they didn't let on. I was filled with a combination of relief and disappointment. Relief that I wasn't about to be made fun of mercilessly (I still can't quite believe it. I don't know if it was the age or the place or the fact that I had exceptionally kind friends) and disappointment because . . . couldn't they see I had LONG hair? Then a couple of days later I noticed Jennifer sporting a black stocking in her hair. Soon, all the girls tried it out, even pinning their own hair up in order to show the stocking hanging down. Joanie went so far as to put panty hose on her head, but we all agreed that was ridiculous.

It was at that time when I realized that I had set a trend. I had an idea that was different; I executed it; and I watched it catch on. It was magical the way we all entered into a tacit understanding that stockings on our heads was cool, even when the evidence should have clearly showed us otherwise. I think I discovered at that moment that fashion was fun and ridiculous, but most important, that as long as I set the trend, instead of following it, I'd be OK.

· · · · · · · · ·

# FASHION
# FAUX PAS
# THAT WORK

I've offered up a few fashion rules in this chapter, but as I've also said, fashion shouldn't be taken too seriously. So as important as it is to know the rules, it's also important to know how to break them. I asked my friend Todd Thomas, a designer and stylist who has dressed such formidably fashionable women as Debbie Harry and Cindy Sherman, for ten classic fashion faux pas that work.

1. WHITE PANTS IN WINTER

2. DIRTY HAIR

3. SILVER AND GOLD

4. NIGHT FOR DAY

5. MIXING SEASONS

6. ROOTS

7. BLUE EYE SHADOW

8. NAVY AND BLACK

9. CHEAP PERFUME

10. TIGHTS WITH OPEN-TOED SHOES

11. CHIPPED NAIL POLISH (YES, NUMBER ELEVEN—TRUE FASHION ALWAYS BREAKS RULES)

This attitude served me especially well as a teenager. My parents kept me on a pretty strict allowance, well past the time I was making more money than any teenager would know what to do with. This was a time before designer cell phones and Juicy Couture. The "rich" kids still dressed like they were slaves to *The Official Preppy Handbook,* that enormously successful guidebook from the early eighties, while other kids tried to spice it up a little by cutting the collars out of their T-shirts à la Jennifer Beals in *Flashdance.* Since I had a limited amount of money to shop with and a lasting fascination with all things nostalgic (especially from the twenties), I started scouring the local vintage stores. I was amazed at the riches to be found. I loved that everything had a story. I would throw on a beaded dress and imagine that I was a flapper in an F. Scott Fitzgerald story; I found a delicate lace dress sheath that actually belonged to Eleanor Roosevelt when she was a debutante. There were men's suits, vests, patterned ties, old seamed silk stockings, dusty dance shoes, lace-up Victorian boots, cut velvet flowers, straw hats. It was all so thrilling.

I especially loved it when I would find a note or a piece of jewelry with an engraving. For years I used to wear an opal ring that my mother bought for me when we were traveling in Australia. It was inscribed *For DL from AJ 1792* in delicate script. I spent a lot of time imagining the love story between DL—Davinia Lovejoy? Dominique Lumiere?—and her ardent lover, Armand Joie—or was it Abraham Jeeves? I pictured them in their final meetings as Abraham was boarding the boat back to England. Abraham scraped up all of his money to buy Davinia this ring and promised that he would be coming back for her. Of course, he never did, and years later, Davinia was forced to sell her ring. There were endless stories such as these—remember, I was a teenager.

Even as my style evolved, it never occurred to me to buy clothing based on what was in magazines (*Teen Vogue* didn't even exist then anyway). I dressed from my imagination, not because of what was or wasn't in fashion. Of course, sometimes in my excitement, I couldn't just choose *one thing*—so I layered. And layered and layered. Around this time, I discovered that I needed glasses. I was, and still am, very nearsighted. I was fond of the kind of glasses worn around the turn of the century; I first saw them worn by the character of Annie Sullivan in a theater production of *The Miracle Worker*, later by Stacey Tendeter in Francois Truffaut's *Two English Girls*. That was the look I went for: simple, round metal frames. The critic Rex Reed wrote somewhere that I dressed like an eighty-year-old bird-watcher in the film *Pretty in Pink*. I was very insulted at the time, but now I think it's kind of cool, and actually kind of sexy. It seems so hard to explain to a teenager how much sexier you are when it doesn't look like you are trying. It makes me proud of my teenage self.

Although the films I made had a costume designer, my personal style heavily influenced the characters I played. I take responsibility for the choices and still stand by them. Well, except maybe the prom dress. (I think I was tired that day.) I would, of course, *love* to have it now, but I was so unhappy with it at the time; it is the one article of clothing that I didn't keep from my wardrobe in *Pretty in Pink*. Same goes for my clothes from *The Breakfast Club*. What I wouldn't give for those knee-high riding boots now!

## LETTING GO

One of the hardest things now is looking at this incredible wardrobe that I have accumulated over the years and realizing that most of it doesn't fit. It isn't just that I'm merely heavier, though truthfully, I am; it's the fact that my body has just *changed*, as bodies are wont to do. Pregnancy tends to do that to us. Even if we lose all the baby weight and then some, our bodies morph into something else. Not necessarily bad, just different. Eventually we have to be brutal with ourselves and look at what we have in our wardrobes, what doesn't belong there anymore, what to keep, etc. This is something I do on a semiregular basis. I have three categories:

1. KEEP. IT'S A STAPLE.
2. DONATE.
3. SAVE FOR MY DAUGHTERS.

This last category, of course, is questionable. I have no idea whether or not they will be even remotely interested in my old clothes when they are teenagers, but I figure if they aren't, one of their friends will be . . . and I'm going to need *some* ammunition to figure out where they are sneaking off to on Saturday night.

Recently I became my own little reality TV show (minus the television) and took a brutal look at my wardrobe to figure out exactly what needed to go in each category. It is truly surprising, and a little disheartening, when you actually look at what you have, what you have been hoarding, what you have never even worn but you keep there so that you won't have to face the fact that it was a stupid purchase or you must have had horrible PMS that day. Or that skirt you can

## BAG THIS

ALTHOUGH I MENTION THE TOP-TIER DESIGNERS, THERE ARE WAYS TO ACHIEVE THE SAME LOOK WITHOUT HAVING TO FORK OVER THE DOWN PAYMENT ON YOUR CAR. LOOK AT WHAT THE DESIGNERS ARE SHOWING THIS YEAR ON STYLE.COM, THEN CHECK OUT WHAT IS BEING SOLD AT MORE REASONABLE MIDRANGE STORES SUCH AS ZARA OR CLUB MONACO. ALSO A FAVORITE OF MINE IS TOPSHOP. EVEN TARGET HAS VERY FASHIONABLE OPTIONS THAT OFFER AN EXTRA BONUS OF ENCOURAGING YOU TO TAKE A FEW FASHION RISKS, SINCE YOU AREN'T INVESTING YOUR 401(K) ON A CUTE LITTLE PATENT LEATHER CLUTCH.

just zip up, but if you wear it, you will have those little horizontal creases and will spend the entire night pulling it down. There is little that makes you look less confident than pulling down your skirt all night. That and chain-smoking are pretty much neck and neck. If you do both, you may as well just give up and call it a night.

If you really want to go the whole nine yards when confronting your wardrobe, I recommend enlisting a friend. There are also services, of course, that offer this sort of thing, but I'm all for recruiting your friends. You can make it a friend date, but be sure that you offer something in return for all her help. Relationship advice, chocolate, a bottle of wine, dinner afterward: it's only fair that your friend be rewarded for slogging through decades of fashion faux pas. As for which friend to pick, choose the one who has the style that you most admire. Lure her (or him) over. In fact, if you have a stylish gay friend, skip the girl and go for him. Odds are he'll have a more discerning eye and will also be tougher on you. Trust me, that's what you need. You don't need to be pussyfooted around. You need tough love here.

Sometimes it's hard for us to get beyond what we paid for a certain item and just accept that it has no place in our wardrobe. If you come across a really amazing dress that is just hopelessly out of style, or is made from a fabric that hasn't kept as well as you would like, try to remember all of the great times when you wore the dress. Did you wear it the first time you went away for a weekend with your boyfriend? Great. Did you wear it that time you ran into your ex-boyfriend at that party and was thrilled knowing for a fact that you looked hot? Savor the memories. Maybe someone took a photograph. Either way, let it go, and forget that you paid full price and half your paycheck for it. Look at it like a really fantastic rental, a sweet convertible Porsche you splurged on for a weekend. Or if that doesn't excite you, choose another car, or an entirely different analogy altogether. The point is—move on.

## YOU ARE NOT A BILLBOARD

While we're on the subject of what to get rid of, I'd like to make an initial suggestion without having seen your wardrobe. My personal pet peeve: T-shirts with logos or advertisements on them. There is nothing that looks quite as sloppy and, well, unfashionable as wearing a T-shirt that announces someplace that you've been, a restaurant that you've eaten at, or worst of all, a phrase that you think is *really* funny (I'M HOME CAN I GO DRUNK NOW?). I don't mean to stand in judgment of anyone here, and as a former T-shirt hoarder, I speak from experience. Not so long ago I had to clear out drawers and drawers full of such T-shirts—some of them given to me by friends but most of them embarrassingly purchased by me. While on vacation, I often succumbed to that inexplicable desire to return home with a medium-size all-cotton memento. To add insult to injury, these shirts rarely fit well, so on top of having BARBADOS! emblazoned across your chest, you're also wearing the style equivalent of a pillowcase. Oh, and I know what you're thinking: *I don't have to get rid of it. I just won't wear it out of the house. I'll only sleep in it!* Let's examine this strategy a little further. Is this really what you want your significant other to see before lights out? You, in an oversize T-shirt hanging to your knees that says BIG BOY MAKES YOU SAY OHHH BOY!

And just because it's a gift doesn't mean that you have to keep it either. (You didn't eat that fruitcake, did you?) When someone close to you brings back a T-shirt to show you that they were thinking of you while they were away (or more likely, they were thinking of you at the airport in the last-minute scramble not to return empty-handed), smile gratefully and then head straight to Goodwill the next day. At times, this sartorial editing must also extend to your kids. Every couple of months, my in-laws like to send a little something for their eldest granddaughter, a little gift to let us know that they are thinking of her. Since Mathilda had been going through a cat phase for quite some time, my mother-in-law picked up a T-shirt that I'm sure she thought was just perfect for her little *agape mou*. CATS OF GREECE it read in big cartoony letters at the top, with colorful drawings of nine cats below.

"Oh, it's so sweet," my husband and I cooed at first glance, reading the titles of the different cats featured. ROMANTIC CAT. SHY CAT. SILLY CAT.

"Aw, she's going to love this," I said—just as my eye happened upon cat number four: STONED CAT. Followed by SERIOUSLY PISSED-OFF CAT. And the clincher: HORNY CAT. In my mother-in-law's defense, her spoken English is far superior to her written English.

A week later, we got a call from her. "Did little Erinoula get the T-shirt?" she chirped.

"Oh, yes," my husband assured her, not wanting to hurt her feelings.

I held up the T-shirt and pointed at Horny Cat.

"I'm not going to tell her," he said, after he hung up the phone. "What's the point?" Besides, as he aptly pointed out, her broken English isn't really at fault here. Who was the weirdo who decided to make a T-shirt featuring "horny cats" in kids' sizes?

OK, my last word on T-shirts. If you still have any of those baby T-shirts with the character drawing and the words LITTLE MISS GRUMPY, or LITTLE MISS HAPPY, or LITTLE MISS CRANKY . . . get rid of them. The expiration date on these shirts is pretty much the day you graduated from high school. I don't care if they still fit you. You may as well be wearing a shirt that says LITTLE MISS I NEED ATTENTION or LITTLE MISS I'M NOT READY TO BE A GROWN-UP. Maybe you aren't, but it happens whether you want it to or not. Trying to look an age that you aren't only makes you look older. It's important to remember that there is a difference between being "youthful" and "youth obsessed."

So how do you dress now? The way I see it, there are few hard, steady rules. The most important thing is to know your strengths. If your legs are the feature that are still kicking, then by all means, go for the miniskirt. If your décolletage is still flawless, then make sure that you invest in wonderful low-cut sweaters and a kick-ass demi-cup push-up bra. Whatever you do, though, stay away from trendy. (In fact, it's a good idea to stay away from trendy at *any* age.) Trendy is a waste of money and takes up valuable closet real estate, as opposed to pieces of real quality that can be worn season after season. It is better to stick with neutrals. It is much easier to mix and match and also makes traveling easier! If you need to, add a flash of color with a fantastic Pucci or Missoni scarf (the Italians are great for accessories).

# A GOOD TAILOR IS NOT
# HARD TO FIND

I still look to the past for inspiration, just as I did when I was younger. As far as I'm concerned, nothing can beat Catherine Deneuve's winter elegance in *Belle de Jour* or the Bouvier sisters' breezy sophistication on the Amalfi coast in summer. But rather than copy these icons outright I like to be inspired by them and figure out ways to reinterpret their style and make it my own. I'm not alone in this approach. I can't say how many times I have found wonderful vintage pieces at antique fairs in NYC, only to learn that extremely well-known designers had already placed a hold on them. Very often they take the pieces back to their studio and literally make patterns off them, mass-producing them as their own creation. And you know what? If they can do it, so can you! Find a fantastic tailor in your area and bring in a dress or jacket that you would like to have remade—perhaps in a more flattering color, or maybe just without the moth holes. While you're at it, bring in your beloved clothing for tweaks before you let it go—the really good stuff. Anything that contains the word *polyester* you can safely toss. Same goes if it has an elastic waist and you aren't pregnant. I don't think that a single article of clothing I wear on my current TV show is "off the rack." Everything needs a little tuck here and there. The very best thing that you can do for yourself is to buy clothes that actually fit you. Not fit the you that you *want* to be, or the you that you *were*, but the you that you are now.

# STAPLES

THERE ARE SOME PIECES THAT I BELIEVE EVERY-BODY SHOULD HAVE IN THEIR WARDROBE NO MATTER WHAT SIZE YOU ARE, OR HOW OLD YOU ARE. THEY ARE THE STAPLES THAT YOU WOULD GRAB IF YOUR HOUSE WAS BURNING DOWN AND YOU HAD TO MAKE A RUN FOR IT. WELL, HOPEFULLY, IF YOUR HOUSE WAS BURNING DOWN YOU'D HAVE MORE IM-PORTANT THINGS TO GRAB THAN YOUR CLOTHING, BUT YOU GET THE IDEA.

## I. JEANS

I think that a lot of people make the mistake of buying jeans that are too light or too tight. And let's not even get into those awful jeans that are prebleached, making the wearer look as if she just sat in a tub of powdered sugar. Unless you're courting a grizzly bear, that look is no good. What you want are the perfect Goldilocks jeans, the ones that fit you just right. Of course, every body is different, so what fits me wouldn't necessarily fit you and vice versa. The best thing to do is determine your body type and match the jeans accordingly. And if there is even a hint of the "muffin top," you know, that roll of fat that spills over the top of the waist, pass them on (and accept that maybe low-riders aren't for you).

Generally it's good to go longer than you think and have them taper gently out toward the bottom. And go darker too. If you have only two pairs of jeans, get one pair that is dark blue and another black. A friend of mine even gets her jeans dry-cleaned, a luxury that most of us don't have the time or money for, but it does extend the life of a great pair of jeans. A good rule of thumb is to remember that skinny jeans should be left to skinny people.

## 2. BLACK CASHMERE TURTLENECK

This is something that I have had in my wardrobe forever. If you take good care of it, it will last a lifetime. Black turtlenecks are the easiest things to grab when you want to look put together but don't want to spend a ton of time putting yourself together. They are incredibly easy to accessorize and to layer in colder weather. In hotter weather, you can forgo the cashmere and go for a silk blend. Cotton is OK, and certainly the most comfortable for hotter weather, but it fades easily, which always makes you look a little . . . well, faded. A black turtleneck looks chic under a trench (a favorite combination of mine—very Yves Saint Laurent) and can also dress down beautifully under a casual jean jacket.

## 3. HERMÈS SCARF

There is nothing better for style or function than a silk Hermès scarf. Truth be told, it doesn't absolutely *have* to be Hermès. There are plenty of other brands out there that fabricate scarves with the same "look," but as far as I'm concerned, Hermès is the top. If you can afford it, go for the best. It was something that I noticed right away when I first moved to Paris, the way that Frenchwomen wore their Hermès scarves—and not just older women. It's like a style talisman that carries women from their twenties all the way into their seventies and beyond, never really going out of fashion. Of course there are many ways to wear your Hermès scarf (see page 40) and there really is no right or wrong way. I like to just fold my *carré* into a triangle and roll it from there, and then around my neck with a knot. If you are too hot, you can always untie it and attach it to your bag. But beware! Hermès scarves are notoriously silky little things, and if you aren't careful, yours might slip away!

## 4. WRAPAROUND DRESS

This dress was invented (or at the very least popularized) by Diane von Furstenberg and is universally flattering for all body types. I consider it a wardrobe staple because, like most women, I tend to gain and lose the same ten pounds over and over again. It's nice to have one dress that you can wear no matter what and still feel beautiful and sexy. Wraparound dresses are so versatile they can even be worn during pregnancy. They are also incredibly easy to dress up and down. Put on a pair of pumps and some clunky gold jewelry, and you are ready to party; or throw it over a bathing suit and wear with flip-flops for a day at the beach.

Most wraparound dresses have a pattern, which are again very flattering to the figure, but choose your pattern carefully. Try to find colors that complement other preexisting pieces in your wardrobe. And if you are a busty girl, invest in a little hook and eye right at the cleavage, depending on how much you are comfortable with sharing with the world.

## 5. TRENCH COAT

Everyone should have a trench coat in her wardrobe. The original was created by Thomas Burberry prior to the First World War, and if you are still looking for one, you would be hard-pressed to find one better than Burberry. However, if you happen to find a snug little vintage Yves Saint Laurent trench circa 1970, thank the fashion gods and never let it go! Take out insurance on it! If you put together an outfit of everything I've listed so far, you have a perfect and chic ensemble. The trench is a wonderful piece to take you from season to season, and of course it never goes out of style. Throw a beret on your head and channel a French Resistance freedom fighter. Change into knee-high leather boots and wraparound glasses and you are *Belle de Jour*. Put one on with nothing on underneath, and you've just given your husband an early Christmas present.

## 6. HANDBAG

Choose wisely. After all, this is something that you will be carrying every day. Try to select a handbag that you won't be embarrassed to carry year after year. Once again, I believe that this is a time when it is better to forgo the trend (e.g., fringe, logos littered all over it, and locks the size of cannonballs) and go for something classic. I have a bag that I bought at Prada in the nineties that looks absolutely modern today. And though I love suede, it will never last the way that leather will. "Scotchgard" it all you want, it will still look soiled after a week. Mulberry and Prada always have the most consistently beautiful and classic handbags, in my opinion. Forget the Hermès Kelly bag. It's a beautiful object but not very practical—particularly the hard-shelled classic. You end up gingerly opening the flap, feeling like you are breaking the binding of a hardcover book, and it barely fits the essentials. The Birkin is more user-friendly but not very wallet-friendly, and the heft of it will send you to the chiropractor eventually. I don't even think Jane carries her Birkin bag anymore, citing back issues. Which really makes one wonder, what does Jane Birkin carry once she forgoes her namesake? A Birkin fanny pack?

## 7. T-SHIRTS

Now that you have already cleared your drawers of all those terrible, messy, oversize T-shirts, you have room for the good T-shirts! Solid colors only, thank you. They are necessary for layering and can also just be worn on their own. And look at how nice and neat they look folded up in your drawer!

I used to be of the mind that the kind of T-shirt didn't really matter, but after being introduced to the T-shirt line of James Perse, I have to say that I am now a convert. The material is the softest and most luxurious imaginable, and the necklines really are more flattering than regular T-shirts. And maybe this is the busy working mother in me talking, but there is something to be said for buying multiples when you find one that you like. It definitely extends the life of the garment and significantly cuts down on the frustration of trying to find that perfect T-shirt again when yours begins to fray.

## 8. A NUDE HEEL

Here's a trick that I picked up from my years on Broadway. Have you ever noticed that the dancers in scores of musicals all have the same shoe? From *Chicago* to *Sweet Charity*. A nude heel really does extend the leg, much more than a darker shade. Pick up a skinny-heeled nude shoe and wear whenever possible without stockings. (Just use a shiny, lightly sparkly lotion for your legs.) You'll add a couple of inches to your height, and your legs will look infinitely better. A couple of decades of dance lessons wouldn't hurt either.

You generally can't go wrong with the high-end shoes (Manolo Blahnik, Christian Louboutin, Jimmy Choos) but your wallet can. These shoes are undeniably beautiful—and crushingly expensive. My friend Julia (who is by trade a costume designer) refuses to spend over a certain amount for a pair of shoes, just on principle. The best thing to do if you want to invest in a great (and expensive) pair of heels is to buy a classic pair at the end of the season on sale, then baby the hell out of them. Make nice with your local cobbler and visit often. Get the tips of your shoes replaced before they actually start to wear down, resoled more often than you actually think you need to, and polished on a regular basis. If you take these preventative measures, you may hang on to your prized shoes longer than you thought possible.

## 9. BLACK BLAZER

Something that always makes your outfit look sharper is a well-fitting black blazer. I particularly love the tuxedo. A black blazer can make you look more finished. You can't get more chic than the famous Helmut Newton photograph of Vibeke Knudsen on a Parisian street entitled *Le Smoking*. Wherever you're living, a nicely well-tailored blazer is a great addition to almost any outfit. For some reason, blazers always seem to be associated with evening wear, but the truth is a good one can easily transition from night to day. Throw it over one of your favorite James Perse tees by day; pair it with a silk halter at night. Incidentally, blazers are a great item to pick up in a vintage store—just make sure you can take out those eighties shoulder pads. And hightail it over to your favorite seamstress to have it perfectly tailored to your body. Too big, and you are revisiting the bad part of the eighties; too small is even worse.

## 10. LINGERIE

Now comes perhaps the most important staple of all: what you wear underneath. You might be thinking, *Oh come on, only my husband sees* . . . and if that's what you were going to say, then stop right there! That is precisely the point! It is all too easy to get caught in an underwear rut, and once you get in it, it's very hard to escape. Beautiful underwear is the ultimate morale booster; it's like walking around with a wonderful secret. The crème de la crème (as far as I'm concerned) is La Perla. Their bras and panties are hands down the most stunning. Not inexpensive, but if you know how to properly wash your lingerie, they last much longer than you think. I suggest getting your husband/ partner involved. Once he sees you in a beautiful set, I'm sure he wouldn't mind donating to the cause. Just make sure that you find a place that knows how to properly size you. Most women haven't sized themselves since they first started wearing bras, and I don't need to tell you that your shoe size isn't the only thing that changes after you have kids! And if you are one of those women who don't think you need to wear a bra, reconsider. Gravity affects us all—not just the Cs and Ds. Besides you don't know what you're missing. You wouldn't think of showing up at a party with a present unwrapped, would you? Think of your lingerie as really glamorous wrapping paper. And you are the gift.

Of course, these are just my top ten staples. There are many more: the pencil skirt with a sexy kick pleat, the boatneck blue-and-white-striped sailor tee, the Converse sneaker (the only acceptable sneaker to wear outside a gym in my opinion). I prefer black, my friend Sara insists on white, but I think that's because she moved to Los Angeles a few years ago. It's true, outside Manhattan, black can seem a bit gloomy during the day. Brown is also a good color, if your wardrobe tends to favor the earth tones.

Keep in mind that different occasions merit different outfits and looks. So much of the pleasure of fashion is putting together the perfect look for a special situation, whether it's a night out on the town with your girlfriends or dinner with your husband at the new restaurant everyone's been raving about. And if you feel like you don't have any reason to dress up, then figure out a reason. Don't wait for one to appear on the horizon; make one up! Throw a dinner party.

The most important thing to remember about fashion, though, is to have fun. Don't take it too seriously. It's easy to be intimidated by the fashion industry, all those photos of gaunt black-eyeliner-wearing models stomping along catwalks, the telephone-book-size magazines declaring the death of one style and the ascension of another, but style is above all a personal issue. Fashion is a chance to experiment, to try new things, to figure out what looks great on you. Approach it with the same enthusiasm that you did when you were young and you were first figuring out who you wanted to be and what you wanted to show the world about yourself.

# HEADING TO THE
# HERMÈS STORE

always feels a bit sacred to me—going to worship at the altar of the god of exquisite taste. But if you don't live near one, eBay is a great place to troll for all things Hermès. Be extremely careful of counterfeiters, however. Read up on the way you can tell a fake from the real thing. But again, I have nothing against wearing something that is not the real thing as long as you aren't *paying* for the real thing.

# HOW TO TIE AN
# HERMÈS SCARF

# IN PRAISE OF THE
# BERET

As with almost any important fashion statement, the
essential ingredient is confidence. This applies to any hat,
but especially the beret. I love the beret because it makes
any outfit look a little sassier, and in the New York winter it
really does keep my head and ears warm—reinforcing my
belief that there is true beauty in function. Things
to keep in mind: avoid red and green for the
political implications. I think it best to stick
with black. It goes with everything and keeps
your outfits from "matching" too much.
How to wear it? Stick it on your head, smush
it to the side, and pull out a few random locks
of hair, and you are ready to go.

# HOW TO PACK
## A CARRY-ON BAG

These days the convenience of air travel has been greatly diminished, not to mention the price gouging that the airlines have all universally instated. Gone are the days when you could essentially fly your entire closet from one place to another free of charge. And anyway, I find it the height of sophistication to be able to pack in a carry-on bag everything you need for a week away. And there is nothing that makes you feel like a seasoned jet-setter more than getting right off a plane and zipping off in a car directly to where you want to go. Here are some tips to packing a successful carry-on bag:

* Roll with it! Forget folding your clothes. I roll everything I pack. It takes up less space, and it prevents unwanted creases.

* Stick to a color palette. Black is the easiest, but in summer, white is just as good. Make sure that your accessories match. For example, when you pack black, don't bother with a brown belt. (Unless you're making a statement. Though I can think of better ones than this.)

* Invest in small toiletry bottles and fill them with your cosmetics instead of lugging the whole bottles with you. You don't need the extra weight, not to mention the fact that with the new security regulations you are only allowed three ounces of liquids on the plane. Many drugstores carry small travel-size versions

of your favorite products as well; it's a good idea to stock up when you aren't traveling so that you have them on hand when you are.

* Pack less than you think you need. The night before, lay everything out on your bed. Put together the possible outfits. (A very type A friend of mine actually goes so far as to photograph her selections.) Make sure you always put something back in your closet.

* Wear your heaviest items of clothing on the plane. They can charge you for any extra luggage, but they can't charge you for what you are actually wearing! Boots take up a lot of room in your bag, so they are a good thing to wear. If you feel that you are going to work out where you are going, you should probably wear your sneakers on the plane, since they are also a bulky item. Layer tastefully. You should still look presentable. The flight attendants really do treat you differently depending on the way you look. You will never get a free upgrade in shorts and flip-flops.

* Make the most of your space. Look at it as a spatial relations puzzle. Find the hidden places in your bag to stash things. Fill your bra cups with socks, your shoes with scarves. If something is breakable, use your sweaters to wrap it up and place it in the middle of your bag.

* Leave room in your suitcase for what you will buy. Most of us always pick up a few things while away. If your suitcase is jam-packed on the way there, you will be forced to buy another bag there to take everything home. If you know for certain that you will buy a lot, roll up an empty duffle bag and stash it in your carry-on. If you don't use it for new purchases, you can always use it to separate your dirty laundry from your clean clothes.

Chapter Three

# BOYFRIEND HAIR, THE SKINNY ON SKIN CARE, AND MAKING UP THAT'S NOT HARD TO DO

HUBERT DE GIVENCHY WAS ONCE QUOTED AS SAYING, "HAIR STYLE IS THE FINAL TIP-OFF WHETHER OR NOT A WOMAN REALLY KNOWS HERSELF." I'm not sure about the exact context of this remark, but he might be on to something. Whether we like it or not, hair is a strong part of our identity. For some, it's right up there with where we're from and whom we love and what we do for a living. And it isn't just women. There's a reason the hair-loss industry rakes in billions of dollars every year. Men are just as guilty of this kind of identification. If you're not convinced, go cut off the nearest slacker's ponytail and watch him burst into tears.

Woman or man, young or old, whoever we are, we tend to treat our hair like a symbol, something between aesthetic decoration and a personal declaration of intent. Nowhere is this more evident than in what I call the "emotional haircut." Whenever something difficult and monumental happens in my life—the end of a relationship, say, or the end of a difficult job—inevitably I will find myself going to get a new hairdo: a new color, a new cut, often both. After spending years growing it out, I'll find myself rushing out to chop it off again, seized by an impulsive and irresistible need to declare to the world, "I'm changed. You don't know the hell I've been through, but here is proof that I am in a different, better place." It's a gesture to ourselves as much as to the world, a hopeful attempt to fortify our spirits.

The easiest and most gratifying hair change is the haircut. But you only get one real shot at it, and then you are in the long and tedious growing game. Of course, there is always the possibility of hair extensions, which these days seem to be about as mandatory in Hollywood as having an agent, trainer, and publicist. But Hollywood doesn't count. This is a place with a long history of artifice. Allegedly Marlene Dietrich used to go to the hair room at MGM studios and have the twenty-four-karat-gold dust shaken out of her wig before leaving work for the day.

Though I have dabbled in extensions, they have always felt like a cheat. The act of growing your hair out requires qualities that you don't need when getting a head full of extensions. (The only quality that you really need for the latter is a couple grand to burn.) Growing your hair out for real requires patience, lots and lots of it, as well as plenty of humility. Every couple of months you go through a stage of horror and dismay, and the temptation to cut it all off is one that I have rarely withstood.

When I was a teenager, the time when we all start making serious statements about our style, I decided that I was not going to be one of those "long hair" girls. This decision was sine qua non, as I had realized the futility of trying to look like what passed for beautiful in Southern California in the early eighties: long blond hair, blue eyes, tawny skin. I figured that if I couldn't look like that, I was better off creating my own look and embracing it. I looked to the past for inspiration. Louise Brooks for the bob in *Pretty in Pink*. A picture of Susan Strasberg for the hair in *The Breakfast Club*. And then one day I saw Jean Seberg in Jean-Luc Godard's *Breathless*, and it was hairstyle love at first sight. I promptly went to the hairdresser with a photo of Jean Seberg clutched in my hand. (I could have just as easily brought a picture of Mia Farrow in *Rosemary's Baby*, but Jean's was first, and it also had the Frenchy expatriot allure.)

"Are you sure you want it *this* short?" my hairdresser asked

"Yes."

"But this volume looks great on you," she said, fluffing my hair into an eighties poof. "You sure you want to lose all that?"

I insisted, and in an hour I lost all of my overprocessed eighties frizz. I had never felt so free and unfettered. By this point in my life, I had become fairly famous and already felt the burden of expectation. Cutting my hair like Jean Seberg's felt deliciously provocative. Even now, I consider this hairdo an expression of extreme confidence. It says, "I like my face so much, I'm not afraid to show it to you." It also says, "I'm not spending an hour with the blow-dryer and hair products," something that most men, ever impatient about women's grooming, should like—although ironically I've found most men don't like the Jean Seberg look.

# BEST ICONIC HAIRSTYLES IN FILM

**Jean Seberg in**
*Breathless*

What else is there to say about this look that hasn't been said (especially by me)? An eternal classic.

**Catherine Deneuve in**
*Belle de Jour*

In a lot of ways, Deneuve is the French version of Hitchcock's classic blond ice queen. Hair back in a twist until she's ravished, and then it's down. Hard to argue with this one.

**Brigitte Bardot in**
*And God Created Woman*

Best example of boyfriend hair there is. Almost impossible to achieve this look without hair extensions.

NEW YORK
Herald Tribune

**Pam Grier in**
*Foxy Brown*
There is no statement quite like Pam's
hot powerful Afro. White people tried to
jump on the bandwagon in the seventies,
but if you don't have the hair or the attitude,
don't bother.

**Faye Dunaway in**
*Bonnie and Clyde*
Long sleek bob, beret optional.

**Rita Hayworth in** *Gilda*
Even in black and white you can
tell this lady is a redhead. She
sports the same peekaboo hairstyle
that Veronica Lake made famous,
but Rita's looks undone and far sexier.

**Yvonne Elliman in**
*Jesus Christ Superstar*
Sexy, long-layered, hippie, windswept
razor cut.

**Louise Brooks in**
**everything**
The inspiration for everything
from *Something Wild* to
*Pulp Fiction*.

I was riding my short-hair high. Most everyone found it attractive—or let's put it this way, no one went out of their way to tell me otherwise. Most people. Years later I ran into Emilio Estevez, whom I hadn't seen in years. We exchanged a mutual rundown of what had occupied us over the years. And then came his parting words to me:

"Never cut your hair short again."

"Um . . . thanks, Emilio."

You never really know how fast your hair grows until you get a short haircut that you would like to keep. (Conversely, you never realize how long it takes to grow your hair until you decide to grow out a bad haircut.) A few weeks after the success of my first *Breathless* homage, I went back to the same hair salon but got a different stylist. I didn't have my Jean Seberg snapshot with me but figured that the hairdresser could just follow the lines of the previous cut. This is a mistake that I have never since repeated. NEVER go to see a different stylist if you are happy with your hair. Hairstylists always like to leave their mark on a style. That's why they are called stylists. Some prefer to be called artists. This one, however, could have been called a sadist. Faster than you could say *Nouvelle Vague* my cute little pixie cut became my "first-week-at-boot-camp" cut or the "I-don't-have-lice-anymore" cut.

"You can *so* pull this off!" my stylist trilled as he sheared my head. It happened so fast! I sat there stunned as I watched the whole look go from cute to severe, from supremely confident to "Don't ask me why my head is shaved, the answer might be sad."

It took all of five minutes. I couldn't say a word, too stunned to speak.

Until he took out the electric shears.

"Please stop!" I cried. "It's short enough, don't you think?"

He leaned on one hip, holding the shaver in his upturned palm like a martini glass.

"I just wanted to clean up all that fuzz on your neck. But if you want to keep it . . ."

"I want the fuzz. Thank you. Please leave the fuzz," I murmured, taking off the cape. "It's OK. I have to go now."

I paid the bill, somehow managing to hold back tears until I got to the car with my boyfriend. We drove around for about an hour while he tried to talk me out of whatever self-destructive thoughts I was having. "You look beautiful . . . You don't look all that different." Somehow his words finally did the trick. Then I made the mistake of stopping by my parents' house on the way home to pick up a dress for an event that I had that night. The reason why I was getting a trim in the first place.

I knocked on the door, since I couldn't find my key. My mother answered the door. She took one look at me and gasped.

"It's OK," she said. "We'll get a wig!"

· · · · · · · ·

# CUT? WAIT . . .

As tempting as it may be to radically shear yourself when a big and difficult moment arises in your life, many of the times you're left afterward still feeling bad—and almost bald. Here are some classic moments in life when it might be better to think twice before reaching for the scissors.

**A BREAKUP:** Perhaps the most enticing time, it can also be the most disastrous. As traumatic as it is to end a relationship, why compound it by tempting the hair gods to leave you shorn and miserable? This is a good time to hold on to your security blanket hair for a bit until you get your pretty back.

**CHILDBIRTH:** Wait until after you lose the baby weight! Especially before cutting bangs—they make your face look fuller, and really, is that the help you need right now?

**BEFORE A JOB INTERVIEW:** Opt for a professional blow-dry rather than an actual haircut. It's not the time for a radical makeover. Confidence is key here, and you don't want to run the risk of feeling like you are someone else.

**YOUR WEDDING:** This is the very worst time to cut your hair! There should be a strict "no-cut policy" in place at least two to three months leading up to your wedding. Those wedding photos last forever, and there are no retakes. This should also extend to your significant other. Unbeknownst to me, my husband took an impromptu trip to an overzealous barber before our wedding. His hair was so short that his scalp was positively radiant—but not in a good way.

It took me years to cure myself of the urge to "Seberg" myself every time a relationship ended, I didn't get a part I wanted, or I was just plain bored. I think it actually took moving to France, learning French, and getting cast as an American in a French movie, *Enfants de Salaud*, to rid me of the desire.

"What deed you do?" the French writer/director asked in horror when I first showed up for rehearsal. When she had met me, six months earlier, my hair had been shoulder length. "Zee hairs were long," she said. "I saw zee character with un chignon. Pulled tight. *Très* severe, you know? Like one of zee American women from CNN."

Not exactly what I had in mind for the character. I was envisioning Godard and his most romantic vision of America, Jean Seberg in *Breathless*. The director was picturing a newscaster. An overly made-up clownish character. A caricature of an American.

"Um . . . I could wear a wig?" I offered, channeling my mom from way back.

"Oh . . . no no no. Zee wigs look not real. Not like zee real hairs."

This, incidentally, is something creepy that the French do. They refer to hair as "hairs," which makes linguistic sense, since the French word for hair, *les cheveux*, is plural. But there is something that just sounds horrible about "hairs." When I think of "hairs" I think of a couple of random hairs, just sort of sprouting on your head or out of your ears. Not a pretty image.

"Ah, OK," she said, shrugging her shoulders exaggeratedly, and blew air from her lips. "So your hairs are short. *Tant pis*."

*Tant pis* is a French expression used ad nauseum to express a sort of vague regret. It isn't a huge deal, nothing to go to the courts over just sort of . . . disappointing. It can be translated roughly as "too bad" or "oh well." I noticed during my years in France that this was a phrase that falls off the French tongue with regularity. It seems the French are disappointed a lot. But on the flip side, they seem to deal with tragedy with the same semiblasé, sanguine demeanor. The most extreme example of this being the story of a friend of mine who ended up adopting the eight-year-old daughter of a local woman who had passed away. The way the young French girl described her life was, "My mother died. *Tant pis.*" I never knew whether to admire the girl's resilience in dealing with her life in such a laissez-faire attitude or to be horrified by it. It certainly made me remember the phrase and to marvel at the wide range of instances with which the phrase could be employed. I don't think the French Revolution could have happened today. Most likely everyone would philosophize about the aristocracy and then shrug and say "*tant pis.*"

· · · · · · · · ·

Right now my hair is longer than it's ever been in my life. I'm alternately proud (what patience!) and embarrassed—embarrassed because of the many conversations I've had with girlfriends about "boyfriend hair." Boyfriends, as we've decided, are suckers for long hair. Sure, you might find the occasional exception—the director Spike Jonze apparently lists short hair as his first requirement for a girl—but, in general, take your average guy and ask him what he likes on a woman and he'll say long hair. My friends and I have argued at length about why this might be, offering up everything from childhood infatuations to hard-core Freudian analysis, from evolutionary biology to biblical narrative (Samson never did get over that haircut, the little baby). Whatever the reason, or reasons, may be, as a woman it's a little disappointing that no matter how inventive or daring you might get in the salon, you're most likely to encounter just a polite shrug from your guy.

"Men are simple," my husband insists. "It's an on-off switch. Long hair is on."

I don't think it's that easy. For me, the analogy is more like a restaurant. Long hair is the thing they're used to, the old favorite, the classic dish. But do they really want to order spaghetti and meatballs every night? Why not branch out? If they would just *try* the veal Milanese with shaved truffles, they would love it . . .

## COLOR THEORY

Somewhere in all of the hair cutting and hair growing there is also the issue of color. I have a theory of hair color that is not unlike my overall theory of life. There is a magical color that you have around the age of five. If you can, never stray too far from this color, either by replicating it exactly—a nearly impossible feat, but a noble one to attempt—or by achieving the *essence* of this color with highlights. Ordinarily I'm wary to espouse any hard, rock-steady rules about style, but I think this one is a pretty good one. There are, of course, always some glaring exceptions to the rule—Marilyn Monroe and Madonna naturally come to mind—but the platinum hair set has its own book of rules and is exempt from these considerations.

At age five, I had a honey-colored auburn that gradually darkened as I got older. When I was thirteen years old, I went to see the original Broadway production of *Nine*, starring Raúl Juliá. There was a number that the late actress Anita Morris performed in a net lace catsuit (created by the brilliant costume designer William Ivey Long), and her hair was stunning. A mass of fiery red. For the rest of the performance, it was all I could think about. Even after the show, I couldn't get the image out of my head, and as soon as I returned to L.A., off to the hairdresser I went. (In fact, I hate to admit it, but I was so bewitched that I ditched school to spend the day at the hair salon.) That afternoon I showed up at home with a head full of Lucille Ball hair. My mother, bewildered by the new bright red me, didn't even think to ask me how I had actually achieved this transformation at school. She just shook her head in dismay.

"You can keep it for a month, then you have to go back to your natural color."

She was true to her word, and in a month I was in the hair salon again, dyeing my hair back. Then I ended up on a film set a few months later where they were trying to decide the look of my character. I was playing a little space urchin-pixie. The background was Moab, Utah, with its stunning copper arches.

"What about red?" I piped up. "Like the color of the mountains?" I added, so as to sound as if I had carefully thought through my motivation.

My hair was changed again that day, and I have never gone back. I'm a redhead, in coloring and personality. My own mother tsks disapprovingly any time I change my color for any reason.

"You are meant to be a redhead," she tells me. "I always said so."

# FINDING THE PERFECT LIPSTICK

## (OR GETTING AS CLOSE AS YOU CAN . . .)

From ancient Babylon to today, women have been fascinated by lipstick. Though the methods of production have drastically changed over the years—rumor has it Cleopatra crushed carmine beetles to achieve her color of choice, while another popular ingredient of the time was fish scales (mmm, kissable!) to add the iridescence needed for that shimmery "disco" look—the desire for finding just the right tint has never waned. Even now, thousands of years since some enterprising woman first smeared carnauba wax on her lips and tried to shimmy past the bouncer at Studio LIV, the quest endures: to find the perfect lipstick.

For years my color of choice was crimson red, partly for the rebel in me that wanted to buck the oft-repeated cliché about redheads not being able to wear red, and also because the perfect red is essentially the holy grail of lipsticks. For a short while I thought that I had found it in a stick that was produced by Shiseido in the eighties, but alas my discovery was short-lived. It was discontinued and regrettably sent to the makeup graveyard along with Clinique's Smudgecicles.

Perhaps it was for the best since as we age it's generally a good idea to stay away from the dark and heavy matte lipsticks and lean toward lip stains, balms, and glosses. Dark lipsticks just make you look older, which is probably why we liked them so much when we were younger! Skip the lip pencil that "matches" the lip color. It's just one extra step that generally makes everything look more severe.

Here are my absolute favorite lip colors that are still available. Make sure to apply sparingly, blot, and don't forget to check your teeth. (Application with cleavage optional . . .)

* CHANEL CRÈME—VAMP
* NARS—BELLE DE JOUR
* CLINIQUE ALMOST LIPSTICK—BLACK HONEY
* YVES ST. LAURENT—FORBIDDEN BURGUNDY
* BENEFIT—BENETINT
* REVLON—CHERRIES IN THE SNOW
* L'OREAL—PINK LADY
* GIVENCHY—BEIGE CHAMPAGNE
* DIOR—SERUM DE ROUGE 510
* SHISEIDO—PERFECT ROUGE RS701

# MY FEW MISGUIDED MONTHS AS A BLONDE

Once in a while, my career decides what hair color I'm to have. A few years back, I was cast in a period piece where my character was described as a cross between Judy Holiday and Marilyn Monroe. A blonde. There was always a suspicion I'd had that I might look good with blond hair. Both my siblings were towheads as children, so I figured that I should be able to carry blond hair. Every time I'd had the red stripped out of my hair and I'd looked in the mirror, inspecting the jaundiced face staring back at me, I'd think, *Well, it's just not the right* shade *of blond—I can't take ash, or yellow. But maybe a* different *shade* . . . So when this part came along I figured it was the perfect opportunity to find out, once and for all, if the secret to blond for me was going to be the shade. I was going platinum. It would be my chance to discover whether blondes really do have more fun.

All I found out from the experience, however, was that blondes need to allow about forty-five extra minutes to do their makeup. I have never felt so self-conscious in my entire life. My brown eyes, which always looked soft and expressive, now looked like little stones wedged into my skull. My freckles, which previously blended perfectly with my various shades of red, looked blotchy and dirty. For the first time in my life, I found myself sneaking out of bed earlier so that my boyfriend didn't see my face without makeup. For the first time I viewed my makeup as a mask rather than as something that discreetly enhances. And the worst part of it was that the same boyfriend (now husband) happened to love redheads, and we had been together for only a month when I went platinum.

Yes, I did get whistled at more by construction workers. But I also had the curiously paradoxical sensation of being invisible. I was like one of those superheroes who watches life from behind a disguise. Instead of the redheaded me that I identified with, there was this strange blond version that received a completely different kind of attention. People spoke to me a little bit louder and attempted to explain things very clearly, as though I wouldn't understand them. It was the first time in my life that I had ever been treated like a dumb blonde. To add insult to injury, there was a young and beautiful natural blonde cast as the ingénue, but it was decided that her character was to be a redhead. She had to deal with the crew mistakenly calling her "Molly" (though she was very good-natured about it). I had to deal with feeling like my identity had been stolen. You never quite realize that you have an identity until you feel that it has been taken away from you.

· · · · · · · · ·

But there are times in your life when you don't want to be you. You want to be new, different, unrecognizable. And each time, I get the same flack from hairdressers.

"But it's your trademark!"

Yes, I know, I tell them—which is precisely why I want to change. For a couple of years when I lived in France I had dark brown, almost black hair. I'm not sure exactly what precipitated this. Perhaps I thought I might blend in a little bit better? I moved to France in my early twenties, hot on the heels of being one of the most recognized people in the United States. Living in a foreign country gave me the kind of anonymity that I hadn't experienced since I was a child. Having a head full of red hair doesn't exactly give you the same sort of anonymity that dark brown hair does. There are times in your life when you want to stand out, and then other moments when you want to blend in and observe.

Inevitably, though, I would feel the urge to get back to myself, and along comes the red hair. It's funny, but I feel that when the red color returns to my hair, it's like I've found myself again. I'm comfortable at last.

Then there is the question of what you are supposed to do with your hair as you get older. In our society, it's tacitly understood that you are allowed to experiment with your hair in your youth, and then at some point every woman is supposed to chop her hair off, let all the hair color grow out, and just sort of de-sexualize herself. Give up on being attractive. Surrender the exotic and the erotic, suspend all effort and interest. I disagree. Not to say that there aren't women who look fabulous with silver hair, but I don't agree with any rules that try to tell us what women should or shouldn't do as they get older. I do think that hair really does represent where we are at in our life. If we are feeling sexy, our hair will reflect it. When it comes to style and self-image, not to mention simple self-assurance, one of the worst things that we can do as women is to announce to the world that we don't care about our hair. So wash your hair. Get those highlights. And stay away from the box color in the drugstore. I promise you, nothing good will come of it.

## MAKING UP
## IS NOT HARD TO DO

With the exception of the few miserable months I spent as a blonde packing makeup on my skin, for the most part I wear next to no makeup in my real life (meaning, my life not spent on the set, or in front of a still camera). I've been asked by various beauty magazines what three makeup supplies I would take to a desert island—which granted is a ridiculous question, since vanity is in pretty short supply on desert islands—but for argument's sake, let's say this is an island that you are marooned on with some cute guy. What three makeup supplies would I bring? A tinted sunscreen, a light lip gloss with a touch of color that tastes really great, and a great pair of tweezers.

The tweezers always surprises them. But eyebrows, believe it or not, are important. The recent brow craze shouldn't be seen as a craze at all but rather the return of something essential that had been inexplicably forgotten. Check out old films from the forties. Those ladies *got* the importance of a good brow. Lauren Bacall's seductive line in *To Have and Have Not*—"You know how to whistle, don't you? Just put your lips together and blow"—granted is a great line, and her lips and hair are fantastic, but in my opinion, it's the brows that really sell it. The brows are what frame the face, and everyone should know how to take good care of them.

Hopefully no one will make the same idiotic mistake I made in my early twenties. My mother always told me, "Never shave off your eyebrows, they will never grow back." I don't really know why she told me this, since who shaves off their brows anyway? Part of me wonders if she hadn't drummed this weird warning into my head, maybe I never would have considered testing it. Why couldn't she have just counseled me against tattoos, like most mothers? So let me tell you, in case there is any lingering doubt: they don't grow back. Or at least, they don't look the same. I shaved mine off—not all the way, just halfway, thinking I could draw them in better. I looked like a demented elf for about a year. And when they finally did grow back in, they were thinner, sparser, like the needles of a Christmas tree thrown out in March. It's never fun when your mother is right about something.

# SKIN CARE

I've given you my opinions on the importance of skin care, but since nothing is quite as persuasive as the opinion of a doctor in a white lab coat (ten thousand TV commercials can't possibly be wrong), I asked my friend who happens to be a dermatologist to weigh in on the issue too. Dr. David Colbert, the author of *The High School Reunion Diet* (high school, again! Can't get away from it . . .), helpfully provided me with his most important tips on how to take care of your skin.

**SUNBLOCK:** Do the "squint test" to determine the SPF: if you can't look directly at the sky without squinting, then you will need an SPF of 15 or higher. Sunblock will protect those fragile-as-cashmere fibers in your dermis called collagen. If you wash that priceless Bergdorf Goodman black cashmere dress in laundry detergent and throw it in the dryer you will basically end up with shriveled shrunken deformed heat-destroyed protein fibrils. Ditto for your skin, ladies. Wear the block—end of story!

**RETIN-A:** Since its discovery over forty years ago it is the one FDA-approved drug that is proven to really stimulate collagen production. A $95 tube should cost $1,000 for the work it does and the money it will save you as the years roll by. My own mother was a Retin-A experiment-in-the-making, starting to use it in the eighties. Now she enjoys flawless skin at sixty-eight and her thirty-two-year-old Argentine polo player boyfriend agrees!

**BETTER LIVING THROUGH CHEMISTRY:** Don't be afraid of scientific innovation. If it weren't for science we'd have never made it past the Plague. That means you should stay up-to-date and use what's available to look and feel younger. That includes a host of lasers, injectables, creams, micro-liposuction, and any new effective technique. Be bold, as long as you are under the care of a board-certified cosmetic dermatologist (not a plastic surgeon, since we don't want you to look plastic).

**LET THERE BE LIGHT:** Repair your reckless-youth, sun-damaged face, hands, neck, and décolletage by doing IPL (intensed pulse light), Fraxel, Titan, or Triads. These are the must-dos to repair your skin from the inside out. They will erase brown spots, red spots, broken blood vessels, and big pores. Guaranteed.

**WEED THE GARDEN:** Keeping your body free of weirdly appearing and persistently hanging little benign growths or skin tags (on the neck, underarms, back, groin, anywhere) is just good skin grooming, as is removing haphazardly appearing brown spots. These take seconds to remove, and it is a painless procedure. Keeping the skin clear helps to keep it young, since many of these growths would eventually take over if given the chance.

**SKIN CANCER SCREENING:** Everyone should have a twice yearly skin cancer screening. Why? Imagine if we could predict breast, lung, or colon cancer before it could spread and hurt us without having a mammogram or a chest X-ray. When it comes to our skin we can see and diagnose skin cancers early on and save lives. There is no excuse not to have all moles checked regularly. That means *all* growths on the skin. The most serious is melanoma, followed by squamous cell carcinoma and basal cell carcinoma. Go to www.skincancer.org and learn what skin cancers look like and how to spot them on you and your loved ones. Do it right now.

I sometimes look longingly at my virgin teenaged eyebrows, but can't get over the amount of makeup I used to wear as a teenager. Was it just me or was it the eighties?

Of course, it makes sense that I would have worn so much makeup as a teenager. Teenagers love makeup, and I was no exception. But the fact remains that the older you get, the less makeup you should wear.

It's hard for me to say this, even now—as far as I've come, I'm still susceptible to the siren's call of a Sephora (it's all the packaging, I swear. Little potions and pots)—but the best advice I could give anyone is to take all the money that they would spend on makeup in a year and invest it in a good dermatologist. And I'm not saying that you need to get Botoxed from here to Sunday, just get your skin in the best possible shape it can be. Did you have acne as a teen? Go for microdermabrasion. Were you a sun worshipper? Get a series of peels. Did you smoke? You can fill those little pucker marks.

Do you still smoke? Quit. This is the time of your life when having confidence is a real asset. If you don't have confidence in yourself, who will? Smoking doesn't look sexy. It reeks of desperation, and it doesn't smell good. Then there's the whole pesky cancer thing. Do yourself, your family, and your older self a great big favor: quit. And then take all of the money that you would have spent on cigarettes in a year and do something fun for yourself. Go on vacation. Buy a new computer. Go shopping at Barneys. If you're buying a pack of cigarettes a day, at ten dollars a pack, that adds up—$3,650 a year buys a lot of cashmere.

Just to make sure that I don't sound too "holier than thou," I'm the first to admit that I was not immune to the smoking trap myself. Much to the dismay of my mother and father, I took up smoking at age fifteen and smoked pretty much nonstop for another fifteen years. I can't say exactly what it was that kept me in smoking's thrall for as long as it did, but it did. What a joy it was to move to a country (France) where smoking was not only tolerated but encouraged. After the antismoking laws were passed in New York City, whenever I was in town I dragged my friends to the same three or four restaurants that tolerated smoking. I ardently identified with the smokers of the world and rolled my eyes at anyone who didn't support my habit. Every time I bought a pack of cigarettes, I couldn't help but feel that I was unwrapping a little Christmas gift in its white-and-gold packaging. I never got over the sordid little thrill.

But as my twenties wore on and the thirties loomed closer, I knew that I would have to quit. Going to see an old movie with a beautiful young woman smoking looks glamorous. Check out that same woman in her seventies. If she still looks good, I'll bet money she quit. If she's still smoking, she probably looks terrible—or she's not around anymore. It's harsh, but there is just no avoiding it. You shouldn't smoke in the first place, but if you happen to get sucked in, hurry up and get yourself free. One day you will have to quit; it's better to do it before you have damaged yourself beyond repair.

Of course, quitting is incredibly hard. I struggled for years to quit, with varying degrees of success. Finally I went to go see a "professional." Mostly, to be honest, I went to get my friends and family off my back. They had stepped up their requests that were beginning to verge on pleading. And a woman whom I adored—my studio teacher for years, Irene Brafstein—lost a very long and painful battle with lung cancer and emphysema. Irene took up smoking as a teenager in Brighton Beach in the forties.

I wish I could say that I saw Irene and quit the next day, but I didn't. It took a bit longer for me to find myself in the "professional's" office. I sat there sullenly and listened as he outlined his system. He charged eighty dollars per session, and he saw people for a total of only three sessions. I was seen for four. He said that I was "resistant," which, upon hearing, I couldn't help but feel a perverse sense of pride. I was no lightweight social smoker, I was the real thing! I can't remember exactly what was said during those sessions, but what I do remember is that he was incredibly adept at knocking down every possible argument that I brought up as an impediment to quitting.

I suggested that maybe I didn't really want to quit. He said that I wouldn't be there if I didn't.

"It's supposed to be harder than heroin," I told him, repeating something that I had parroted over the years.

He shook his head. "It's not. I've worked with both. Heroin is infinitely harder to treat."

"Oh."

"But nevertheless, it is a very strong addiction."

He made me visualize the desire to smoke as an addict living within me. He further suggested that I look at my "addict" as a very wily four-year-old child who was better at manipulating me than anyone else because, well, it was me. She knew all of my secrets. She knew my buttons, my weakest moments. It was up to me, the adult, to keep the little brat in check.

"You wouldn't give a loaded gun to a four-year-old child, would you?"

"Obviously not," I snapped. Then feeling guilty, I added a lame joke. "What, do you think I'm a Republican?"

He ignored me. This guy was not big on humor, but he did have a lot to pack in during those four sessions.

"Well, it's the same thing. Because, make no mistake, it's the same thing. Smoking will kill you."

"But what about all those ninety-year-olds that—"

"They're an exception. Do you really want to be on that side of the statistic?"

He then proceeded to elucidate on the effects of smoking, in lurid, incredibly descriptive, downright cinematic detail. (I later found out that this therapist only saw smokers as a side gig. His "regular" job was counseling terminally ill cancer patients on pain management.) I couldn't help but picture my beloved teacher in her last moments. Irene was put on a list for surgery to treat the emphysema when they discovered the lung cancer in the preliminary tests. When I asked her what it was like trying to breathe with the emphysema, she pointed to one of those little red-and-white straws that you stir your coffee with, the tiny ones that aren't really for drinking, just for stirring. "Try to breathe through that . . . all of the time," she told me.

Somehow it got through to me. Maybe it was the right moment for me. I wish that I could have found that moment some time in my twenties, or even better if I had never taken it up in the first place, but man am I glad that I quit in my thirties and not my forties. I still love it when my husband takes a whiff of my hair and tells me it smells great.

. . . . . . . . .

There comes a point in your life when you are encouraged, however subtly, to stop changing your look. Conventional wisdom tells us, at a certain age, that you should have found your look by now and stopped searching. But the nonconformist in me rebels at the thought of giving up on experimentation in order to prove my maturity. I never thought I'd disagree with Givenchy, but while he was a master of the cloth—and certainly did right by Audrey Hepburn—as a hair psychologist, he had his limitations. "Hair style is the final tip-off whether or not a woman really knows herself." Oh, Hubert, do we ever really know ourselves? We are always evolving. Hair can be as good a barometer of that progression as any. And while there are obvious mistakes that we can learn from (never cut your bangs with toenail clippers) as well as proven successes (I, for one, expect to remain a redhead for most of my life), like anything else, it's all about enjoying the ride. So go ahead. Experiment! Color, curl, feather, flip, tease, and twist and when it's time . . . cut. Because in the end—unlike any other choice you make and will be stuck with your whole life—your hair? It always grows back.

# Chapter Four

# WHO'S **GOT** YOUR BACK?

YEARS AGO I SAT WITH MY FRIEND DARCY IN A BAR IN LONDON. We were discussing motherhood, which had been on the forefront of my mind, since I was in my early thirties and, as every medical journal never tires of screaming at us, once you pass the age of thirty-five it's time to get the show on the road. Darcy announced to me that she had little interest in children and that she suspected she would be happy to remain childless. I brushed off her sentiments and basically told her that she would grow out of it. My friend bristled and, rightly, took issue with my condescension and inability to see anything outside my narrow scope of reference. I wanted to have kids, so I incorrectly assumed that everyone else wanted to. This brief incident embarrasses me even now as I think about it. Fortunately almost a decade later we are still friends. Me, happily married with a family, Darcy happily childless and still holding tryouts for Mr. Right.

How grateful I am now to have friends without children! As much as I do appreciate those with kids—the fact that you can meet any mother on the playground, point out your respective offspring, and boom! insta-quasi friendship—there is nothing like getting together with a friend over a glass of wine and talking about something *other* than your kids. These friends are extremely valuable, and too often these friendships are thrown out with the bathwater.

When I get together with Darcy, our conversation covers a diverse range of topics, from relationships to politics, from books to boys, from my latest projects to her latest students. (Darcy is a writer and recently minted teacher to a few very lucky students.) Children are certainly not off limits in our discussions, but I do find that we end up talking more about ourselves, and I find myself being reminded of the person that I was before so much of my every waking moment revolved around these other little creatures. How easy it is for us to forget ourselves! As my nonparent friends inadvertently remind me, it is up to us to keep it together, to make time for the gym, to take the time to do whatever it is that we like to do, reminding ourselves of who we are as separate beings, apart from the relationships dearest to us.

My own mother made the choice to be a stay-at-home mom and raise her children without the help of a relative or a nanny. I can count on one hand the number of times that we had a babysitter. It happened so rarely and was such a novelty that it felt like a holiday when it did occur. I remember the name of only one of our babysitters: Cherry. How beautiful and glamorous she seemed to me with her long center-parted hair, straight as sheets of glass, and her Bonne Bell Lip Smacker.

Throughout our childhood, we had our mother's clear, undivided attention, and all of us flourished like hothouse flowers. She was a room mother for me and my brother and sister, organizing field trips, decorating cookies, driving us to our swim team practices, Little League games, and dance lessons, as well as driving my father (who happens to be blind) to and from his work as a jazz pianist. In her "spare time," she took a class as a mechanic so she could service our car, a used 1966 turquoise Rambler. She expertly sewed our Halloween costumes, Easter dresses, school play costumes; baked her own bread; preserved the fruit and vegetables from our garden; cooked meals (a different one for each child, since our tastes varied); and read us a bedtime story every night. She always stopped at a crucial moment in the narrative, just when she knew we were hooked, announcing that it was "lights out," and then she

would hide the book—I remember my brother, Kelly, and I searching all over the house for *Island of the Blue Dolphins*, never managing to find it. Every night was a treat. As far as I was concerned, my mother was Superwoman.

Years later, after we moved from our smaller town in Northern California to Los Angeles, where rents ran three times what they did up north, my mother decided that she needed to get a job to supplement our family's income. Since she married right out of high school and never attended college, she went to a temp agency to find out what kind of a job she could get.

I was at home when my mother returned, after walking around all day in heels that she was unaccustomed to. (My mother stopped wearing heels and skirts some time before I was born. I can never picture her in a skirt, just as I can never picture my father without a beard.) She entered quietly, holding the heels in her hands.

"How did it go?" I asked, excited. I was twelve years old, and the thought of my mother doing anything outside the family seemed positively exotic to me.

"I'm unqualified," she said, shaking her head. "It seems I'm unqualified for anything. Anything at all."

I watched her heartbroken as she trudged back to her bedroom and closed the door. This was my mother. My mother who could do *anything*.

· · · · · · · · ·

"The problem," my mother says now, "is that I picked a profession that becomes obsolete. I always knew that I wanted to have kids and be a homemaker . . . but I never counted on you kids growing up. You have to have something outside of your children, you know? They didn't tell us that back then. Or maybe they did, but I didn't hear it."

It seems strange to me now when I think of how both of my parents impressed upon me the importance of having a career—any career, as long as it is something that I loved. Additionally, they encouraged me to have pursuits outside it, things that could nourish me and help keep me from placing too much importance on my career. Why then didn't she follow her own advice and ensure she had other sources of nourishment? Part of it, certainly, had to do with her upbringing—she is a member of a generation renowned for its stoicism and self-sacrifice—but the rest is still a mystery to me. I asked my mother what she thought she would do after her children grew up.

"I didn't think about it."

Didn't think about it? How is that possible? This is a woman who scrupulously budgeted, counting every penny for our family, a woman who began saving for our college education the second we came out of the womb. How is it that she didn't think about herself? When I was the last child to leave the nest, my mother fell into a huge depression. All the years spent thinking and caring for everyone else had finally caught up with her. She entered therapy for the first time, and as she says, she cried nonstop for two years. The therapist, a kindly woman, fifteen years my mother's senior, nodded her head in agreement. Life was hard, hers harder than most in many ways. She passed the box of Kleenex and then said the same thing she always did, "*What are you going to do about it?*"

It took a couple of years, but at the age of forty-eight, my mother went to a culinary institute and perfected something that she was already good at. She made friends, went into business with my father, and ran a successful catering business on the side. The depression vanished. Was it the schooling? Was it succeeding at something for herself? Was it making friends? My mother insists that it's the electrical shock she accidently gave herself when she was crossing over a field at her sister's ranch in Petaluma. "That electrical shock fixed me right up!" she swears. "And I didn't even have to pay for it!" Yes, it's true that my mom loves a good bargain, but she also has a great sense of humor.

· · · · · · · ·

Although my mother now sees her friends with some regularity—going out for dinner, taking in shows at the Sacramento playhouse, where my parents buy seasons tickets, along with their friends—I can remember a time from my childhood when it was rare for my mother to spend time outside the family.

In this, she is far from unusual. There is something that happens in every woman's life. It starts in middle school (sometimes even earlier) and then is repeated at various times, with varying degrees of intensity, over the years. The dumping of friends for a relationship. I have perpetrated this on my friends as the "dumper" and also been the "dumpee," finding it suddenly impossible to get my friend on the phone after that friend has exchanged a mutual "I love you" with his or her significant other. Once that happens, you can consider yourself dumped. At least for a time.

The most extreme case of dumping occurs when one has a baby. After you have a baby, the days of straight-up spontaneity are pretty much behind you until you send your kids to college. After my first daughter, Mathilda, was born, my social life came to a grinding halt. Every moment I didn't spend with her or at work, I spent catching up on sleep or trying to figure out a way to make my body look like it did before. (Which, in my case, seems an impossible feat. I find myself looking at other actresses of my generation in the magazines and thinking, *I must have gone to the wrong celebrity school. Why do their stomachs look* flatter *after having had children?*) In any case, every moment that I spent away from my daughter felt "stolen" and undeserved.

At the other end of the spectrum, however, there is nothing like a baby to help justify *not* doing all of the things you need to do to take care of yourself. Maybe other people have always been better about dividing their time, but it took me a while to realize that I was a better mother when I took the time to recharge my batteries. I am more energetic when my body is healthy. I am happier when I find the time to enrich my brain—when I actually read the books on my bedside table. When I go to an off-Broadway play. When I just sit with a friend over coffee for half an hour and talk about nothing.

Sometimes I miss the days of heading out into the street and not knowing exactly where I'm going, running into a friend at a neighbor-

> I DON'T UNDERSTAND HOW A WOMAN CAN LEAVE THE HOUSE WITHOUT FIXING HERSELF UP A LITTLE—IF ONLY OUT OF POLITENESS. AND THEN, YOU NEVER KNOW, MAYBE THAT'S THE DAY SHE HAS A DATE WITH DESTINY. AND IT'S BEST TO BE AS PRETTY AS POSSIBLE FOR DESTINY.
>
> —COCO CHANEL

hood café, drinking wine in the afternoons (admittedly, this is something that seems to be hard at *any age* unless you live in Europe). It's an oxymoron, but we need to *plan* for spontaneity with our friends. We know about the importance of "date night" with our significant other, so why not also have a date night with our friends? It isn't easy, but your friendships will thank you for it. Pick a day (or night), depending on your job, and trade off deciding what you are going to do—even if it's just going to see a movie, hitting the sales at Bergdorf's shoe salon, or getting your nails done. The time spent with a friend is invaluable. You need it, and your friends need it too. It is very exciting when your friends have babies, but when you are the one without children, it can become disheartening after a while to always be rescheduled, postponed, put off. It is important to remind your friends that you are still you, just as it is necessary to remind yourself.

That being said, the one place that I think should be avoided as a "date with friends" idea is the gym. Yes, it's good to have a gym buddy—I know that I benefit from a little bit of healthy competition—but dates with friends should be spent doing something you both *love*. If you both love bench-pressing, by all means, party on. But most of you probably are closer to me. When I think of what constitutes a good time, aerobics, StairMasters, and chin-ups have absolutely nothing to do with it.

Date night with friends is about indulging yourself. One of the reasons for the massive success of a show like *Sex in the City*, other than Sarah Jessica Parker's undeniable charisma, is that it promoted dates with your friends. There is something that we get from our female friends that we can't get anywhere else. There is a firsthand knowledge that they have. You don't need to *explain* everything. One thing I love about getting together with a girlfriend is the fact that they know *exactly* how PMS feels. They will never try to tell you it doesn't exist, but by the same token, a girlfriend will never assume it's "that time of month" if you are acting erratic or feeling morose. Girlfriends will never lie to you if you ask them to honestly tell you if you look fat in those jeans. In fact, a really good friend will tell you without being asked, and it's never embarrassing or degrading when a girlfriend tells you this. Somehow it's OK to be objectified by a really good friend, 'cause you know it's for the greater good. (Of course, good girlfriend etiquette demands that you also are informed when your butt looks really cute in those jeans.)

Sometimes life intervenes and it is absolutely impossible to spend time with your friends. For example, I think that there is a six-month grace period after you have a baby or adopt. Other times, life just takes us in wildly different directions, and we have to accept it and let those friendships go. And as painful as that can be, sometimes they miraculously come back to us.

· · · · · · · ·

When I was six years old, I entered at a new school. I didn't know anyone there. I had recently recorded a jazz album with my father's band, which brought me all kinds of attention in the local jazz community, and pretty much ensured my freak show status at school. There were two older boys who would track me down daily and taunt me, imitating my little squeaky voice from the record. *How had they even heard it?* I would wonder. *How did they know the lyrics?* Whenever I saw the boys coming, I would look down and run in the opposite direction.

Near the end of my first week of school, a little girl with long blond hair and blue cat-eye glasses came up to me on the playground. She was holding my album in her hands. I tensed up, fearing that I was about to be teased.

"Hi! I'm Jenny! Would you autograph my album?"

She handed over a clearly well-played LP. I took it and signed "Love, Molly" with little musical notes sprinkled around my name.

Jenny and I quickly became best friends. She would come over to my house after school and join me when I performed with my father's band at local shows. We would have slumber parties at her house. (Incidentally, it was Jenny's older brother Douglas who was my chief taunter at school. Mystery solved. But in his defense, it must have been beyond aggravating to a twelve-year-old boy to have to listen to the thing as many times as this record seemed to have been played in their house.) Jenny and her five siblings and numerous cats and dogs lived in a wonderfully cozy home. Her parents made the choice not to have a television. Jenny's mother says now that it wasn't so much a choice as a decision not to buy another one after their TV broke. "I never realized it could be so quiet until it broke and we didn't have to listen to five children argue over which channel to watch!" The television was hardly missed. There was no shortage of things to do at the house. There were always plenty of art supplies around, and the backyard was full of interesting diversions—Jenny's father was a collector and restorer of Pack-

ard automobiles. The whole family was remarkably academic, and all of them have grown up to be doctors, lawyers, and high-level political consultants.

One day when we were seven, Jenny and I were in the backseat of my family's car, talking about what we were going to be when we grew up. I stated emphatically that I was going to be an "entertainer." I was going to be a famous singer and actress. There was very little doubt, as far as I was concerned. Jenny thought this was a good idea. Then she announced that she was going to be a nurse. This seemed like a good idea to me too. My mother glanced at us in the rearview mirror and said, "But why a nurse? Why not a doctor?" My mother still likes to claim credit for Jennifer becoming a successful ob-gyn—never mind that she was top of her class at Berkeley, ditto Stanford—my mother thinks she can trace it all back to that fateful conversation. Who knows? Maybe she's right. Jennifer doesn't discount it.

When my family moved away, Jenny and I tried to stay in contact. She would visit me in Los Angeles, I would visit her occasionally in Sacramento, but eventually our lives became too separate. By the time we were teenagers, I felt that we had little in common. We barely spoke anymore. We didn't have a big falling-out, we just sort of gradually fell apart. I acted in a movie when I was nineteen where I played a pregnant teenager. There was a scene where my character took a sip of champagne at a family get-together. When the film was released, I received a very angry letter from my friend (who was in premed at the time), telling me how irresponsible the scene was and citing numerous statistics in regards to fetal alcohol syndrome. I felt unjustly accused and started many letters to Jenny telling her so, though ultimately I never sent them. Instead, I decided to simply let it go. What was there to say? We had definitely grown apart.

Losing a friend can be painful, especially if it is acrimonious in any way. My friend Meredith cites losing a close friend of hers as the single most painful event of her life. She had a friend in college she was so close to that they were almost like one person—finishing each other's sentences, confiding every thought and secret. After the friendship ended, Meredith felt like a part of herself was missing, as if she had a phantom limb. I asked her if she ever tried to find someone to replace that one special friend.

"I couldn't," she says now. "I don't even know if I would want to. I find myself parceling out bits of information to many different friends, rather than just one. Maybe it's just a defense mechanism, but it's what I do. If I want to talk about books, let's say . . . maybe I'll call Panio. Cooking . . . I'll call Jane. I don't think I'll ever give that much of myself to just one friend ever again."

Sometimes we have to let our friends go and trust that if we are meant to get back together, we will. Otherwise we learn to cherish the time that we had together and know that nothing that we do has to diminish those memories. And sometimes our friendships do find their way back to us, or else we find our way back to them.

At the beginning of my thirties, I faced something that I didn't know how to handle. Even now, I don't really know how to talk about it. A late-term miscarriage. That's the short way of saying what happened to me. It would take a much longer and heavier book to properly explain what it was and how I felt. Suffice to say, I was desperate. Desperately sad, confused, and terrified that there was something terribly wrong with me and that possibly I would never be able to have children. All of my doctors in New York City seemed incapable of explaining to me what had gone wrong and, worse, equally incapable of reassuring me that it wouldn't happen again. Well-meaning friends handed out platitudes such as "It's nature's way . . ." I wanted to scream at them, "What do you know about nature and her ways? Go write a Hallmark card where people actually want to read things like that." I wanted *real* answers.

One late night, a few weeks after it happened, I found myself calling Jennifer's parents—recalling their number by heart. I felt like I was six years old again. They miraculously have the same telephone number they have had since I met her in 1976. They gave me her number in Michigan where she was practicing obstetrics, and within minutes I was on the phone with her and telling her the story, bawling my eyes out. She calmly listened, took my medical history, and wouldn't get off the phone with me until she was sure that she had uncovered every stone, examined every possible avenue, and left me with enough hope to believe that in spite of this, I would carry another baby to term—that I would be a mother. She put me in touch with other doctors in New York whom she trusted. I have to say, there is nothing quite as comforting as having a friend that you have known since you were six years old take your medical history.

Since then Jennifer and I have been in regular contact. Even though we don't live in the same state, there is a bond and mutual respect that will never be broken. And when we do see each other, we get to watch our daughters play together—her eldest with little cat-eye glasses and long hair, mine, tall and lanky with big brown eyes—there is no better feeling.

. . . . . . . . .

The older we get, the harder it can be to make new friends. Not impossible by any means, but certainly trickier. When you are a kid, it seems like the easiest thing in the world. I sometimes watch my daughter enviously when I see her make friends on her school's playground in the simplest way. A curly-headed blond girl with the most adorable lisp sidled up to her one morning and tapped her on the shoulder.

"What's your name?"

"Mathilda. What's yours?"

"Elle."

"I like cats," my daughter told her.

"Me too. Let's be friends!"

"OK."

And off they went, holding hands, skipping across the yard to discover what adventures they could uncover.

Boom. This was the extent of their introduction, and they have been best friends since. No baggage. No history. No expectations. That all comes later. If we could just figure out a way to hold on to that simplicity. But marriages, family, responsibilities, careers, and our own personal histories get in the way. In short, *life* happens.

So how do we make friends as adults? The first step is, obviously, having the desire. Very often we get stuck saying to ourselves that we are too old. The time for making new friends has passed. We treat friendship like a new language—if you didn't pick it up in middle school, it's too late. Why bother? This is far from the case. One of the advantages of being older is that you know yourself better—you know what traits really matter to you in a friend, and what you have to offer to a friendship. You can embrace your differences, rather than trying to fit a mold. A Mohawk isn't going to convince anyone over thirty that you're a nonconformist.

While it's fundamentally about having the right attitude—a willingness to put yourself out there and meet new people—a change of venue can help. Sure, it's easy to make friends at work, but then when you meet up after work, guess what you talk about? Better to branch out a little and see if you can't find a friend who offers a new and interesting perspective on things. A lot of people I know have met some of their

closest friends while pursuing an activity. Whether it's a cooking class, a language workshop, or a regular game of dodgeball (a friend of mine is a team captain!), surrounding yourself with people who share your interests and are bold enough to take risks is a terrific recipe for friendship. It doesn't always work, of course, but when it does it can offer a remarkable and unpredictable boost to your social life.

Being a celebrity, of course, complicates friendship a bit for me—not to say that it makes it impossible, but there is always the odd and undeniable fact that many people know me before I know them. Or at least they know some *version* of me based on a movie they saw me in, or else a grossly inaccurate, un-fact-checked Wikipedia entry. It can throw the most down-to-earth people for a loop, trying to figure out how to act— how to see me as the woman I have become rather than as the public person I have been almost my entire life. I am so grateful to those who get it right.

# FRIENDSHIPS THROUGHOUT HISTORY

SUSAN B. ANTHONY &
ELIZABETH CADY STANTON

HANNAH ARENDT &
MARY MCCARTHY

ELIZABETH BISHOP &
MARIANNE MOORE

DOROTHY PARKER &
ROBERT BENCHLEY

GLORIA VANDERBILT,
OONA CHAPLIN &
CAROL MATTHAU

JACQUELINE KENNEDY &
LEE RADZIWILL (FRIENDS
AND SISTERS!)

BABE PALEY & SLIM KEITH

# BEWARE OF THE
# UNDERMINER!

As inspiring as good friends can be, there is nothing quite so demoralizing as a bad friend. Often, however, they slither by undetected, discreetly ruining your life. A friend of mine, Mike Albo, wrote an entire book on the phenomenon of the "Underminer," a friend who is dedicated—either seriously or casually—to making you feel terrible about yourself at all times.

Here are some of Mike's expert tips on how to spot your very own "Underminer":

Your Underminer is *strangely hotwired into your soul*. He/she can detect even the tiniest whisper of doubt or regret that you harbor. If you are feeling unsure or insecure about something, you can bet your life that your Underminer will bring it up, delicately, with a moony look of concern on his/her face. "That's great about your raise. Now what about your capacity for love?"

*Overuses the word "Fun!"* when describing your achievements and appearance. "Wow! Your show was really fun!" "That skirt you wore last night was so fun! On you!"

The Underminer *thinks he/she is the world's expert on your happiness*. When rehashing a recent night, your Underminer will make sure to tell you how "happy" you looked, as if you are usually living with constant depression. "I was watching you talking last night at the bar and you looked so happy, holding your Bloody Mary."

The Underminer *always puts on a good face for others* around you. New friends/coworkers/romantic possibilities invariably LOVE your Underminer when they meet him/her. The next day, your Underminer will probably tell you some cryptic fact about the new person that you did not know. "Your new girlfriend is so sweet and intelligent! It was great to talk to someone else, finally, about Burmese politics."

To highlight your lack of success, the Underminer *casually mentions successful people and connects them to you* in the guise of a compliment. "That new actress reminds me so much of you, like ten years ago." "Did you hear that amazing piece on *This American Life*? It reminded me so much of that idea you had for a short story."

In social settings, the Underminer *brings up fleeting, embarrassing styles or opinions from your past*, especially if you are with someone new who doesn't know you very well. "That's so weird that you're gushing about Berlin right now, because didn't you always say you kind of hate Germans?"

If something unfortunate happens, the Underminer will *make sure you know he/she always knew, secretly, that it would happen.* "It's too bad Franklin broke up with you. Everyone thought he was so great for you, but I always knew he was sort of a sociopath."

Your Underminer is likely to *reveal himself/herself at any moment you are feeling elation.* Be on the lookout when you get a promotion, new haircut, second date, or are about to leave for a trip. "I love your new tight hairstyle. Did you also get a chem peel? No, no, it's just you look so much . . . smoother."

I realize that it isn't easy. While I am fairly underwhelmed by celebrity myself, I do confess to spending an entire Toronto-to-New York flight sitting next to Leonard Cohen without ever mustering the nerve to talk to him. I almost managed to squeak out my undying respect for him as a writer/poet/singer when, just then, the flight attendant swooped in and knelt at his feet like Mary Magdalene. She proceeded to swoon over him right up until it was time to fasten our seat belts and put the tray tables up. I eavesdropped and listened to him respond quietly, graciously to her questions, but I could hear the fatigue in his voice and couldn't ignore the open *Toronto Times* in his lap that he was in the middle of reading. I decided to leave poor Leonard alone and retreated back into my book for the brief remainder of the flight. But who knows the opportunity I missed? Maybe Leonard could have been my new BFF?

## MY FACEBOOK SPACE ODDITY

In the past couple of years, countless "social networking" sites have cropped up like little mushrooms in the forest. Being the proudly tech-savvy geek girl that I am, I have embraced these sites—under assumed names of course. Although there do seem to be quite a few pseudo–Molly Ringwalds out there. (Don't be fooled. I would *never* choose that wallpaper!)

Sometimes it's hard to imagine life before Facebook and MySpace and Twitter and the countless other sites vying for our membership. How did we ever keep up socially? What a great way to stay in contact with friends! Thanks to the latest batch of updates, I know that my friend Merritt is heading out to Morton's Steakhouse for a "very special dinner." My friend Iris is "overworked." Naomi "killed a massive black widow with a stick." But what do I *really* know? At times, it feels like having CliffsNotes friendships. I have a vague idea of where my friends are in the world but no idea of how they are actually feeling. A huge majority of friends update their status when they are drinking a cocktail after a "lonnng day." But we never hear how or why the day was long. It's always just enough information to give us the illusion that we are in contact.

I've recently come to the realization that these networking sites perhaps hamper friendships more than they help them. The little "tweets" seem to satisfy our curiosity enough so that we put off getting together—after all, they come daily, even hourly at times. Additionally, every status update is intended for the world at large (or at least the massive list of "friends" that you invited in an elementary school flashback desire to be popular). Consequently, people rarely ever say what is really going on. When is the last time you shared that you are sad because you got in a really huge fight with your husband? Or that you were fired? Or that you are just depressed and don't know why? Social networking sites are meant to be light and funny and glib. They are a performance. They have somewhat replaced the after-work bar experience—but it's BYOB, and no one's going home with anyone.

Before our twins were born, some real (non-cyber-space) friends threw a party for my husband and me to celebrate the upcoming birth. There was something so refreshing and relaxing about sitting down with people, in the flesh, and telling one another stories. Being able to touch them, to hear their laugh, to look in their eyes. I had such a wonderful glow going all day and night, as did my husband.

"We have really nice friends," he said during our walk home.

"Yes, we do."

"We really should make a point to see them more often."

"Absolutely," I agreed.

"We need to find the time."

That's really what it comes down to, isn't it. Time.

But in the meantime I will log on to Facebook tonight just to find out if there is anything new. Darcy saw an iguana the size of a basset hound cross the street in Costa Rica, and Alona needs stamps but hates walking to the post office. Marci is having a yard sale, and Thomas forgot how loud thunder can be. Kim is "giving up on perfect . . ."

# FOUR FRIEND DATES

**BOOKSTORE:** Time to channel your inner librarian. A great way to connect with anyone is through a wonderful book. Make a date with your friend to meet at your local bookshop and pick out a book to read together. Treat it as a sort of book club for two. Even if it takes you years to read the selection (Um . . . Gaddis anyone?) it can only strengthen your bond, seeing the different ways you relate to the book and how the book, in turn, relates to your lives.

**BOTANICAL GARDENS/BEACH:** In the stress of our modern-day lives, sometimes getting together with a friend can seem like another task to be completed. When you are feeling depleted, why not to go someplace where you can just be swept away by beauty. I love the botanical gardens—particularly when the cherry blossoms are in season. Nothing really seems to be too bad when you have pink petals fluttering down around you.

**CLASSES:** Not only are classes a reliable way to make new friends, but they are also a fun way to enrich your existing friendships. Foodie friend? Try a cooking class featuring the cuisine from a country you both fantasize about visiting. Fellow theater lover? Go take a Broadway dance class and learn all about Fosse "jazz hands." (Yes, they do exist.)

**WINE TASTING:** This one should be reserved for the post-work/weekend hours. Wine tasting is both a lovely way to spend a couple of hours with a friend as well as a fun way to learn about wine so you don't have to rely on the ubiquitous *Wine Spectator* number plastered on every bottle in the supermarket. If you are a teetotaler? Go pick some berries instead. (No judgments here!)

*Chapter Five*

# SHE GIVES GOOD E-MAIL

I HAVE ALWAYS BEEN WHAT CAN BEST BE DESCRIBED AS A SERIAL MONOGAMIST. Ever since my dating history began, at the age of fourteen, there was always one special person . . . until there was the next special person, usually six months to a year later. Rarely did I ever date two people at once, though I fully approved of the idea. It just went against every fiber of my being that was screaming "Meld! Meld!" like a deranged Vulcan—if you'll excuse the *Star Trek* reference.

The turnover from special person *de jour* to the next was fairly dependable. To this day, I tend to chart important happenings in my life to what guy I was dating at the time (or, alternatively, what hair color I had). My driver's license? Michael. The day I moved into my first house? Adam. And so on . . . I was never really stressed-out about finding Mr. Right. I figured that all of them were right—until they weren't. There were a couple of stinkers thrown in there. "Knickknacks," my mother calls them. "You and your sister have always had a taste for knickknacks," she would tell us, shaking her head. But for the most part, they were all decent and had their own various charms going for them. I can usually look back and see where I was coming from; I can see why that particular person attracted me at the time. I can also understand why they don't now.

My curious method of charting time came to a halt when I got together with someone in my early twenties and stayed with him for close to a decade. I no longer found my memories so easy to differentiate—they all were wrapped up in this one man. The relationship ended just as I was turning thirty-three, the moment when you *are* thinking about Mr. Right . . . or more specifically, Mister Give Me a Baby *Right Now!* Like many women, I never really thought about the timeline for having kids. I just knew that it would happen when the time was right. Then bam! I was thirty-three years old, leaving a long relationship and marriage, and realizing for the first time that the certainty that I'd always had was suddenly eluding me.

It was just my luck that the first person that I fell in love with, post breakup, was a twenty-five-year-old man. A brilliant writer and black belt in tae kwon do—"You could do laundry on his stomach," my friend Helena enthused to me about him before we had even met. In fact it was Helena who was initially smitten with him, as she moaned to me about the relationship, which was going nowhere. At that time, he was twenty-four. "What are you doing with a twenty-four-year-old?" I sniffed. "What could you possibly have to talk about?"

It was sometime later that I met the man myself (without actually realizing that it was the same person). Helena had recently formed a little "Pre–Facebook and MySpace" online group, something between a contact list and an e-literary salon. Every day she sent out a bit of poetry, along with a paragraph of whatever novel she happened to be reading, to a small group of writerly types. Everyone was supposed to respond with a piece of something great that *they* were reading. She cleverly named it "Quip Pro Quo."

Since I was still reeling from the dissolution of my marriage, having a little bit of daily inspiration in my in-box became something I looked forward to. One day I found a stunning piece of writing by John Cheever. It was the last paragraph from a story entitled "Goodbye, My Brother." It took my breath away. I wrote to the person, thanking him for contributing it. He wrote back, telling me that he appreciated the Stephin Merritt lyrics I had contributed the previous week.

OH, WHAT CAN YOU DO WITH A MAN LIKE THAT? WHAT CAN YOU DO? HOW CAN YOU DISSUADE HIS EYE IN A CROWD FROM SEEKING OUT THE CHEEK WITH ACNE, THE INFIRM HAND; HOW CAN YOU TEACH HIM TO RESPOND TO THE INESTIMABLE GREATNESS OF THE RACE, THE HARSH SURFACE BEAUTY OF LIFE; HOW CAN YOU PUT HIS FINGER FOR HIM ON THE OBDURATE TRUTHS BEFORE WHICH FEAR AND HORROR ARE POWERLESS? THE SEA THAT MORNING WAS IRIDESCENT AND DARK. MY WIFE AND MY SISTER WERE SWIMMING—DIANA AND HELEN—AND I SAW THEIR UNCOVERED HEADS, BLACK AND GOLD IN THE DARK WATER. I SAW THEM COME OUT AND I SAW THAT THEY WERE NAKED, UNSHY, BEAUTIFUL, AND FULL OF GRACE, AND I WATCHED THE NAKED WOMEN WALK OUT OF THE SEA.

—FROM JOHN CHEEVER'S "GOODBYE, MY BROTHER"

Thus began our e-mail romance, a flirtatious correspondence that lasted for close to six months until we finally met face-to-face.

Our initial meeting was a bit disorienting, to say the least. Because of his decidedly foreign name and impressive vocabulary (not to take away from his academic accomplishments, but his first language was Greek, which honestly gives you a leg up) I was fully expecting a short and swarthy intellectual type. A guy with wild hairs growing out of his eyebrows and mismatched socks. I had no idea that this was the twenty-five-year-old with washboard abs that my friend had been swooning over. His e-mail was his full Greek name, as opposed to the shortened version that he regularly goes by—which explains my confusion, as well as my total lack of adhering to the girl code of "Thou shalt not date the obsession of thy girlfriends."

When I complained to my friends about the fact that he wasn't at all what I had pictured, I got everything from a raised eyebrow to a generous helping of an arch gay friend's sarcasm: "Cry me a river, Molly." It did seem silly, but more than my long-held reverse snobbery regarding obviously good-looking people was the blatant fear staring me in the face. How in the world was this twenty-five-year-old going to be in any way interested in starting a family in the next couple of years?

In the early days of our pillow talk, I would try to glean as much information without seeming too obvious. "What's your favorite color? Baby blue? Aw that's so sweet . . . If you could be any animal . . . a cheetah? No kidding . . ." And then I snuck in there like a ninja. "And when might you like to have kids? What? Sometime in your FORTIES?" I've never been good with math, but a quick calculation put me squarely in the land of busted biological clocks. Early forties for him meant late for-

# DATE PLACES

When choosing a destination for a date, it's good to keep
a few key considerations in mind.

**FIRST**, pick somewhere that has lasting potential, as it's
disappointing to return a year (or more) later for an anniversary only to
discover that it's been demolished and replaced with a T.G.I. Friday's.

**SECOND**, make sure that it's personal.

· · · · · · · · · · · ·

Anyone can whisk someone off to a fancy restaurant—it's generic
and a little obvious. Try for something unique instead, someplace
that's unexpected and memorable and will show a revealing and,
hopefully, interesting side of you. (Incidentally, that doesn't mean
you should totally forgo fancy restaurants; just make sure there's
a reason you picked it. For example, you visited Spain once and
have loved tapas and sangria ever since.)

· · · · · · · · · · · ·

One of the things I find endearing is when you are taken someplace
that makes you feel separate from the world. If it's during the day and
you are sufficiently outdoorsy, hike to the top of a mountain. If you
happen to be in New York City, channel Deborah Kerr in *An Affair to
Remember* and head to the top of the Empire State Building. "It's the
closest thing to heaven you can find in this city."

· · · · · · · · · · · ·

Not to put too much pressure on any fledgling romance, but if one
of your favorite films of all time is playing at the local movie house,
why not just put him to the test right away? I mean, do you really
want to spend your life with someone who doesn't see the merit of
Michelangelo Antonioni? (Or from my husband's point of view, classic
kung fu films. I confess I nearly failed this test, since I literally passed
out during a viewing of Jackie Chan's *Drunken Master 2*.)

ties for me, which meant . . . no babies. No way, no how. It seemed like an obviously doomed future. I decided to regard him as my "getaway car," the fun speedy little number that you drive across the panhandle, get good and dusty, and then ditch at the border. I even halfheartedly attempted to set him up with a young literary girlfriend of mine (which I'm happy to say, he nixed, telling me firmly that he could find his own dates, thank you very much).

I'm pretty sure that in some way I was attempting to control the situation as much as possible, to control the heartbreak myself, like a Band-Aid that doesn't hurt as badly when it's you that does the pulling. But all glibness aside, we know that the heart has ideas of its own. I was falling in love with someone who was in another phase of his life entirely. (I do believe that our lives are lived in seven-year cycles. A concept summed up neatly by the Jesuit missionary St. Francis Xavier, "Give me the boy until the age of seven, and I'll give you the man.")

Which has always begged the question in my mind: Why did my youth make all those older men I dated feel young? Being with a younger man didn't make me feel younger. Quite the opposite. It made me feel older. It shined a light on all of my experience. It made me self-conscious about my body, for the first time, and it honestly took me years to stop saying things like, "Well, you probably don't remember Devo . . . but they were really big in the eighties."

What do you do in this situation? The reality is that by the time we get into our thirties, and definitely in our forties, we are beholden to the choices that we made earlier on, before we knew better. Most people are in their forever relationships already (or on their second or third forever relationships). And most men, surprise, surprise, are attracted to younger women. I know, because for many years, I *was* that younger woman. Being the older woman all of a sudden was a role that I was unaccustomed to. It seemed to happen just like that—all of a sudden. And I don't think that I'm the only one for whom it's happened like that. You are the youngest person in the room, and then bam! You're not. And sometimes, depending on the situation, you're the oldest.

This predicament was particularly hard to deal with, since I had always been the go-to girl for all of my friends for dating advice. Especially for my friend Eloise, who had hands-down the worst dating history of anyone. We met when we were both in our early twenties in New York, and we hit it off immediately. She was smart, beautiful, creative, funny, the only daughter of artistic, highbrow parents. It confounded me as to why, as the years ticked by, Eloise remained single. I think the answer dawned on me around the same time that I realized it was a good thing that she no longer drank. Since I love wine and adore sharing a beautiful bottle with close friends, it always irked me that I had a really good friend who couldn't drink at all.

"Not even a little teeny bit? Just a taste?" I'd wheedle during lunch.

Eloise would shake her head. "You don't understand," she'd say as we waited for the check. She gestured to my wineglass. "You see that little bit you have in there, left at the bottom? It would be all I could do not to lunge for that, and drink it down before we left. It would torture me that you left that. In fact, it's been years now since I've had a drink, and it still kind of tortures me."

Years later, as we got to know each other better, I realized that the same impulses that governed her alcohol (non)consumption were at play in her devastating dating history. She went after men with the same single-mindedness and intensity of an Amazonian spear fisherman. And the men responded exactly the way I imagine the fish do. The few that she managed to spear were very short-lived—usually just hookups.

"Men are hunter-gatherers," I continually reminded her, sounding like a fifties sociology textbook. "They like a little mystery." Eloise, however, seemed absolutely incapable of holding back when someone caught her fancy. And *everyone* caught her fancy. She was able to read romance into everything and everyone. Even the postman could be a viable suitor. After all, he brought her letters and packages *every day*.

Things reached a feverish peak when it became clear that she was getting to the age when the window on baby making was rapidly shutting and there was no candidate for fatherhood in sight. After watching her solicit every eligible man in Manhattan for his sperm, it got to where I was afraid to leave her alone with *anyone* of the opposite sex, lest she bring up her "project." She visited my family over Thanksgiving one year under strict instructions not to bring it up. In the morning I discovered she had hooked up with my brother.

"Well, you said I just couldn't ask for his sperm, right? You didn't say that I couldn't sleep with him!"

She at least had the dignity to look a little sheepish. Her quest for reproduction took her to far and unexpected places. She solicited every gay friend, old school chum, an ex-flame's best friend (which I always thought was a little sketchy, since they were going for it "the natural way"—some friend!). The search culminated with a man she met on a culture trip to Cuba. She somehow got him to agree to "donate" his sperm and found various reasons to go back and keep trying, no small feat, given the stringency of the laws at the time. Her considerable efforts, however, ultimately met with no success.

"Well," she mused, during one of our late-night chats, "he does only have one testicle. That might have had something to do with it."

"What!" I practically screamed. "You have been flying back and forth to Cuba, spending a fortune on tickets, breaking laws, to become impregnated by a guy with ONE BALL?"

"He has a fake one. But it's incredibly lifelike," she offered. "You know, I wouldn't even have known unless he told me . . ."

. . . . . . . . .

Eventually it got to the point where I told Eloise to talk to me before every date so that we could discuss areas of conversation that should be off limits. In addition, she would forward her e-mails to me, and I would do my best to decode them and help craft a response.

"You should have a dating column, a sort of 'Dear Abby' for our time," Eloise would enthuse. "You're so good!"

Mostly I would give her time limits on how long to wait before she could respond. None of this, however, led to any improvement. This confounded me until I found out later, through mutual friends, that all of the suggestions and tips I gave her—what I considered to be thoughtful, practical, well-seasoned dating advice—went unheeded. No matter how many times I instructed her to let the guy make the first move, I

# FIVE THINGS
## TO DO (OR NOT DO)
# AFTER A BREAKUP

**PACK IT UP.** Take everything that reminds you of your now ex–significant other and put it in a box. Wrap strong sticky tape around it. This last detail is very important, since it can be tempting to bust it out and torture yourself after drinking too much wine. The tape is usually a pretty good deterrent—depending on how much wine you have actually imbibed.

*DON'T* **DRINK TOO MUCH WINE.** There is a saying that there is no problem that can't be made much worse by drugs and alcohol. I'm all for wallowing—it is an essential part of the grieving process; however, an excess of any mind-altering substance can keep you from genuinely feeling your feelings. Everything becomes a little bit better or a lot worse. The only thing that can heal you is to honestly deal with the pain. Better to do it with a clear head and leave the wine to the good times.

**START A RIGOROUS WORKOUT REGIMEN.** There is no better time to get into shape. It will do wonders for your fragile ego (and no one's ego feels great during a breakup—no matter who is breaking up with whom). Mix the high-intensity cardio with relaxing and centering yoga.

**PLAN A TRIP AWAY WITH A REALLY GOOD GIRLFRIEND.** Make sure that you don't pick a place that has too many memories attached to it. One day when you are stronger you will want to reclaim those places, but now isn't the time. Pick a place that you have always wanted to visit but were vetoed in the "Where should we go on our vacation?" discussions. Take lots of pictures of you looking gorgeous. (If you don't feel gorgeous, act like it anyway. Your brain will eventually catch up.)

**IMAGINE THE POSSIBILITIES.**
Think of every interest that you have ever wanted to pursue but have never found the time, then try a few. I bet we would be very surprised if we added up the countless hours that were spent on unhealthy, destructive relationships. A Buddhist adage says something like: "If you weren't thinking about that which makes you unhappy, what *would* you be thinking about?" So think about it. Whenever you feel caught up in the misery, stop and ask yourself what you could be doing with that time instead.

would hear otherwise, like the tale about her trying to talk a man she had just met at a wedding into pulling over into a motel during the drive back. I threw up my hands after a failed relationship with a guy who founded one of those Internet travel sites. "It's never going to work if you don't listen to me!" I'd holler.

"It's OK," she assured me, after the guy cheated on her with his ex-girlfriend. "I told him that I would forgive him if he gave me the gnome." She holds this souvenir—a garden gnome from a travel site's advertising campaign—among her other treasures: early Ramones tickets from the eighties, original scribbles from her old friend Andy Warhol, and Jonathan Larson's notes from early drafts of *Rent*. Eloise definitely has a taste for knickknacks.

· · · · · · · · ·

Some of my other friends aren't quite as laissez-faire about the dissolution of a relationship. Another of my girlfriends, Marie, has had her share of relationship mishaps in the past. A tall, ravishing redhead with impeccable taste in everything from home décor to food to garden design, Marie is a culture snob of the highest order, but with the goods to back it up. Her crisp South African accent only serves to add to her chilly allure. And yet in the years since we met, I witnessed one heart-wrenching breakup after another.

"How could Marie *possibly* be single?" I pondered aloud to a male acquaintance of mine. "She is easily one of the most beautiful women I have even seen."

"Maybe she is more attractive to women than to men," he said.

It was a puzzling comment, but I figured that he was just responding to her temperature—her unreachable hauteur, perfect posture. Her habit of wearing all white all winter without so much as a smudge. The way she always had an umbrella when it rained, along with the perfect trench. Her guaranteed ability to know the perfect, obscure wine pairing for every meal. All qualities that women admire—certain traits that we aspire to, the way that we read fashion magazines, thinking that somehow if we buy the clothes and the makeup then we might actually be able to look like that one day.

The last time that Marie was single is the last time I attempted to be a matchmaker. My husband and I were friends with an artist who had gone through his own recent heartbreak. He was successful, attractive, and a very close friend. One night after dinner I mentioned to my husband how great it would be if we could set them up.

"It'll be perfect!" I insisted. "*She* loves art. *He's* an artist. She loves to *cook* amazing food. He loves to *eat* amazing food . . ."

"I don't know," my husband said, ever the voice of reason. "What happens if it doesn't work out?"

"Oh they're grown-ups!" I said, pooh-poohing his lack of enthusiasm. "I mean think about it! It's always such a crapshoot when our friends get together with someone. Isn't it a better idea to stack the odds in our favor? We like both of them already! It's ideal!"

My husband rolled his eyes. "Whatever it is that makes you want to do this, whatever gene it is . . . I don't think I have it."

"It isn't a gene, it's gender," I called out over my shoulder.

I was already off to the kitchen to set about organizing a dinner party to make the introduction. When it comes to romantic setups, I always feel that it's better to have a few people around, rather than overtly double-dating—which puts way too much pressure on the prospective pair. Blind dates, meanwhile, are just awkward and cruel for everyone involved. And in the spirit of full disclosure . . . I admit that I like to be there to survey my handiwork—there's just that little bit of control freak in me. Either I have a God complex, or more likely a yenta complex. *Did.* I have to remember this is all *past tense.*

For the dinner party I prepared a beautiful beef bourguignon the day before, letting it simmer for hours, and then transported it, along with all of the other culinary accoutrements, to our artist friend's apartment. It was a magical evening, plenty of good food and wine along with intelligent conversation, set against a wintry Manhattan backdrop. The dinner was a resounding success. Our friends started dating almost immediately. I felt very proud.

"You see?" I boasted to my husband. "O ye of little faith."

"Yeah yeah yeah," he said. "Just wait. It's just the beginning."

The relationship seemed to flourish, though there was an obvious underlying tension. Marie, like most women I know, tended to push for immediate intimacy, while our friend escaped into his work whenever things got a little too intense.

I held counsel with Marie. My husband got the male point of view. "This is going to come to no good. I know it," my husband predicted.

The first breakup was about six months in. Then they did what all sadomasochistic urbanites do—they got back together, to see just how much pain they could inflict on each other. A year later, while my family was traveling across the country, our friend broke up with Marie a day before her birthday. When Marie e-mailed me to tell me the news, I did what any sympathetic friend would do. I fired back a quick reply, commiserating with her, elucidating my friend's (now her ex's) faults, and why she was better off without him.

Little did I know that Marie, in a fit of fury and rage befitting the ancient Greeks, took on a little Martha Stewart do-it-yourself project. She put together a compilation of the *worst* e-mails that she had received about him, with choice words from her mother and her friends (including yours truly). These were forwarded to him in a tidy document with a virtual bow tied around it—his complete character assassination as a little memento to remember her by. I learned two important lessons from this Sturm und Drang. (1) I will under no circumstances try to fix any of my friends up, no matter how wonderful they are individually or how forlorn they seem around Valentine's Day. (2) I will look long and hard at that "send" button before I press it.

Did this sort of drama happen in our twenties? Certainly. But the way we felt about it was different. Getting broken up with at any age sucks, to be sure, but the sting we feel in our teens and twenties feels like an annoying little nibble from a gnat. We wailed and made really great mixed tapes full of bitter songs featuring the Smiths or Elvis Costello, but in a couple of weeks, we were on to the next. Getting dumped at thirty-six just feels like it has more weight to it. A nasty mosquito bite—like the ones that get you in the summer that swell for days. The closer you get to forty (if we continue with the insect analogy), it is more like a bee or a wasp sting. You feel like if you don't have the Epi-Pen on you, you just might die.

So what do we do? Many women respond to the idea of being single at this point in their lives with complete and utter panic. They have poor judgment, they lower their standards, they dress inappropriately.

# THE JOYS OF BEING SINGLE

Marriage and kids are great, but as many of my single friends can attest to, it isn't the only way to be. There is an unquestionable stigma attached to being single in our society, though there shouldn't be. I admire my friends who have made the choice to "go it alone" and confess to twinges of jealousy when comparing their personal freedom to my carefully structured time-managed existence. Here are some great aspects to being unattached.

1. THE ABILITY TO TRAVEL ANYTIME, ANYWHERE WITHOUT HAVING TO SYNC UP YOUR SCHEDULE WITH ANYONE ELSE'S.

2. NOT HAVING TO SWITCH OFF HOLIDAYS TO BE WITH "HIS" FAMILY OR "YOUR" FAMILY.

3. BEING IN CHARGE OF THE REMOTE.

4. HANDING *BACK* THE CHILD (AFTER HE OR SHE CRASHES FROM THE SUGAR HIGH).

5. FLIRTING WITH WHOMEVER YOU CHOOSE.

6. PSYCHIC SPACE.

7. MORE TALK ABOUT SEX—LESS ABOUT REAL ESTATE.

8. SANCTIONABLE SELFISHNESS.

9. MAKING AN "X" IN THE BED.

10. FALLING IN LOVE AGAIN.

At their worst, they drag their children through their bad decisions. This sort of panic has to be looked at as akin to a bad acid trip. You are not thinking clearly. You need to wait for this drug to make its way out of your system. (Granted I have never actually dropped acid myself, but I've seen *Trainspotting* . . . or was that heroin?) Anyway, the point is we need to not make choices based on fear. Sometimes the best thing to do after a long-term relationship ends is to step back and let yourself heal. Don't just fling yourself back into the dating pool without taking care of yourself first—odds are, you'll just end up belly flopping. Don't worry, the dating pool isn't going anywhere; it'll still be there when you're ready for it.

· · · · · · · ·

I knew a woman in her midthirties who, much to her unwelcome surprise, suddenly found herself succumbing to a kind of blind panic when it came to relationships. She suffered from the prettiest-girl-in-high-school syndrome—which I personally think is the worst thing that can happen to a woman. It sets you up for a world of disappointment, a sad sort of determination that as an adult, all of your best years are behind you. Far better to be the geeky girl with glasses and braces. There's nowhere to go but up. It reminds me of a gorgeous actor that I worked with. He was stunning. Cheekbones that could cut glass, olive skin, thick shiny hair. But strangely, his personality didn't match his looks at all. He was kind and honestly humble, without a trace of disingenuousness. It intrigued me. One day I came right out and asked him. How could he be so good-looking and so, well . . . nice. He answered as bluntly as my question. "I had terrible disfiguring acne as a teenager."

So the prettiest girl in high school grew up and spent all of her time trying to recapture the high that she felt when she was a teenager. All of her focus went into her appearance—making sure that she hung on to the only thing that she felt mattered. You could say that her choices in men became increasingly as shallow as her obsession with her façade. But only focusing on your appearance is a fantastic recipe for depression. Especially since as we age, we need to face the fact that our beauty changes. That's not to say that older women aren't beautiful; we are. We just don't look like we did when we were teenagers. And depression leads to the very worst kind of decision making. My friend bounced around from one miserable relationship to another, eventually finding herself dating a man who collected Nazi pith helmets and owned two enormous female (and very possessive) potbellied pigs—which he insisted sleep in the bed with them at night. She told me that as she lay in bed at night, listening to the pigs snore, she wondered what had become of her life. How could her standards have fallen so low?

The imperative is not to get down on yourself, since that inevitably leads to the dreaded D&D (and I'm not talking about Dungeons & Dragons). The dreaded D&D are Depression and Desperation. Desperation is like the antipheromone. Men can smell it wafting off you like a bad odor, and it is a definite turnoff. The whole myth of men wanting to take care of us is just that, a myth. Not to say that in a perfectly healthy relationship, a man wouldn't want to provide for you—but the key here is "healthy." It isn't very often that a man will meet a woman who is depressed and desperate and say, "Hmmm, a basket case. I want that!" More likely he'll run for the hills.

# WHAT DO YOU MEAN BY THAT?

The rules have definitely changed since our mothers' generation. Just the fact that we are even writing about e-mail (which didn't exist) and its attendant etiquette is evidence that it's a brave new world. But while technology has radically changed, human behavior hasn't. There is nothing quite as maddening—and maddeningly familiar—as meeting someone, liking him, exchanging personal contact information . . . and then waiting to see how it all plays out. If he contacts you first, then great. Mystery solved. But as we know, nowadays it is perfectly acceptable to make the first move. What happens afterward, what you do—or don't do, and when—is where the trouble can often start. Here is a guide to help you decipher the intricacy of the male of the species and his primitive, habitually mystifying e-mail response.

(Admittedly, since you have already read how I got together with my husband, this is clearly a case of "do as I say, not as I do." I will say that I learned from my mistakes.)

# TIME THAT IT TAKES FOR HIM TO GET BACK TO YOU AND HOW TO INTERPRET IT

**ONE WEEK:** Hopefully you've met someone else during this week, because on this guy's list of priorities, you are beneath laundry and cable bills.

**TWO TO THREE DAYS:** Long enough to be discouraging, but not so long that you can definitely write him off. If you really like him, remember that anyone can get caught up with the exigencies of life. That being said, if there are a couple of these in a row, forget him.

**NEXT DAY:** He could be a guy who likes to take his time, which if you think about it, isn't such a bad thing. Look carefully at the content. If it's a long, newsy e-mail, it's good. If it's short and cursory, chances are he's just being polite.

## ONE HOUR: THE SWEET SPOT. HE CLEARLY DIGS YOU.

**FIVE MINUTES:** What, doesn't this guy have a job?

**ONE MINUTE:** He's a stalker. Run!

And if a man *does* seem to prefer you when you are down, then that should be a big red flag for you that this guy likes control. I once dated a guy who couldn't have been happier when I was down—which forced me into the trap of downplaying my triumphs lest it bruise his fragile ego. Much better to be with someone who loves you all of the time but encourages the best part of you, rather than the worst.

· · · · · · · ·

Have you ever noticed how women are their most attractive just after they have fallen in love? There is something that happens that relaxes the face, you laugh more, you are happy, you emanate a warm confidence. When you're single, the trick is to find that confidence in yourself *before* you fall in love. To do this, what you need—and this may sound corny, but it's true—is to fall in love with yourself.

I know that I feel at my best when I am active both physically and mentally. As counterintuitive as it may seem at the time, when I work out I have more energy. When I write, even if I feel that I have nothing to say before starting a session, I end up with an enormous feeling of accomplishment, which in turn feeds my ego (and believe me, my ego likes to be fed). And I am happy when it is *me* doing the feeding, and not someone else. I have a nice love-hate relationship with my ego. I know what a pig she really is, but I love her anyway.

One of the things that can really wear away at your sense of self is when you find yourself doing work that you can't stand. If you are in a dead-end job that is killing your soul, then take steps to get out of it. It can't happen overnight, it could take months—or even years, if it involves going back to school—but even doing research on what kind

of job could make you happier is a step in the right direction. Getting on an exercise regimen when you are overweight and out of shape may seem like a lost cause, but it isn't. You just have to remember to stick with it. If you do, you will begin to see results. There is no way not to. (Unless you cheat and eat a box of Ho Hos in front of the TV at night. When it comes to getting in shape, diet really does matter. There's no way around it.)

Another way to fall in love with yourself is to become involved with a charity. Find something you feel passionate about, whether it's homelessness, marriage equality, literacy, AIDS, it doesn't matter, and see what you can do to help. There are plenty of worthy causes, so don't just assume that there's nothing that fits your type. It could be saving your local community garden. Being a Big Sister or Big Brother. Just find something that gets you out of yourself, that takes you away from your seemingly insurmountable problems. Even donating just a little of your time can go a long way—not only for the cause, but also for the wonderful feeling it can enkindle in you. Doing good for someone else is an incredible high. You may even find that you are so good at what you are doing, and you feel so great doing it, that it helps you find direction in your life. It might give you hints about a new career that you should be pursuing (if you are stuck in an unsatisfying job). The important thing is to immerse yourself in something other than finding love. Nine times out of ten, love finds you.

And when you do find someone who catches your eye, and who catches yours back, do yourself a big favor. Make sure that he isn't married. Sure it's possible to fall in love with a married person and actually end up together (after an alternately thrilling and miserable, guilt-ridden courtship), but this is the exception to the rule. What usually happens is that the unmarried person is strung along for as long as she allows herself to be, and then the guy tearfully confesses that he can't leave his wife. Don't invest in these junk bonds. Even if you do decide to make a go of it, the karma will surely bite you eventually—if not in this life, then in the next.

· · · · · · · ·

Another thing to watch out for is the casual hookup. Now I don't consider myself an uptight, reactionary woman. I love sex. There. I came right out and said it. (Sorry, Mom!) I only suggest you hold back a little for strategic reasons. There is something so delicious about waiting. It's foreplay! I will never understand why anyone would want to take away one of the best parts of courtship. And however much you think you would enjoy getting down on the first date, just imagine how great it would be by the third or the fifth. I'm not saying to hold out forever, but delayed gratification has been proven to reap many benefits. Look at the marshmallow experiments conducted by Walter Mischel at Stanford University. Scores of children were put into a room with marshmallows placed in front of them and told that if they waited and didn't eat the marshmallow for twenty minutes, they could get a double helping after the wait was over. (If you haven't seen the film, watch it on YouTube. It's a classic!) The marshmallow experiment is pure torture for the four-year-olds, but it's fascinating to see how they each handle it, the inventive (and to any adult, painfully familiar) behavioral strategies they come up with to fight the craving, whether it's turning around in their chairs so they can't see the marshmallow, or talking to themselves, or just angrily kicking the table in frustration. Years later Mischel followed up to see how the kids were faring as teenagers. The evidence was overwhelming. Every kid who was able to delay gratification was also more successful in every way compared to their marshmallow-devouring counterparts. Those who delayed gratification were found to have far greater emotional intelligence, did better on their SATS, and were generally happier. I think we can all learn something from this. Next time you find yourself falling in love—picture him as a marshmallow. Wait until at least the third date to sink your teeth in.

I took this principle to the extreme when I got together with my husband. Our courtship was delightful and almost entirely over e-mail. In fact, he is the first and only boyfriend with whom that happened. It was a truly modern courtship, yet there was something lovely and old-fashioned about it. We got to know each other through letters—it was downright Jane Austen-ish. Then I went and screwed it all up by panicking about the age difference and my need to extract a promise from him that he would be ready to have kids in a couple years. My thinking was that I didn't want to invest in someone who was going to turn around after a few years and say, "You know what? Kids aren't really on my agenda." It makes perfect logical sense, but strategically it was a disaster. And if I'm being honest, I was a bit hysterical—and not in the fun, wacky Lucille Ball way, more in the Isabella Adjani *Story of Adele H.* kind of way. (Adele H., the daughter of Victor Hugo, became obsessed with a British naval officer, and her deranged stalking ensured that he would have nothing to do with her.)

During this difficult period, I waited by my computer and pressed the "refresh" button more times than I care to admit. If five minutes passed without a reply, alarm bells went off in my crazy brain and I fired off a frenzied e-mail to him, diagramming our relationship (mind you, we were still in the first six months). I harassed, harangued, cajoled, and emotionally blackmailed. He told me later that he spent so much time talking me down off my cyber-ledge that it was nothing short of a miracle that he didn't get fired from his job. In my lunatic state, I don't think I ever stopped to consider that he had a job. In short, I did everything that I would counsel a friend not to do. "Stop it!" I would tell her. "You'll scare him away!" But it's hard to see clearly when you are out on that ledge.

# IF MUSIC BE THE FOOD OF LOVE, PLAY ON

We've all been there—probably more than once. There are few things worse than a bad breakup. There is nothing to do but pack everything is boxes (or burn them in a ritual ceremony if you really want to purge), call good friends, but most of all, listen to music really loudly, and cry, just as loudly. Here are some of my favorite breakup songs ever. They range from the knife-in-the-heart despair to the empowered "Guess what? I never loved you anyway"—all sentiments that you are likely to be feeling at the same time. Listen, wallow, and repeat.

## BREAKUP PLAYLIST

* "I'M LOOKING THROUGH YOU"—THE BEATLES
* "I CAN'T TOUCH YOU ANYMORE" —THE MAGNETIC FIELDS
* "NO CHILDREN"—THE MOUNTAIN GOATS
* "GOOD WOMAN"—CAT POWER
* "I NEVER WANT TO SEE YOU AGAIN"—QUASI
* "THEY'LL NEED A CRANE"—THEY MIGHT BE GIANTS
* "SO SAD ABOUT US"—THE JAM
* "YOUR EX-LOVER IS DEAD"—STARS
* "BABY, I DON'T CRY OVER YOU" —BILLIE HOLIDAY
* "OH WHAT A DAY"—INGRID MICHAELSON

* "CRY ME A RIVER"—(JULIE LONDON VERSION)
* "THESE BOOTS ARE MADE FOR WALKIN'"—NANCY SINATRA
* "DORY PREVIN"—CAMERA OBSCURA
* "MEANINGLESS"—THE MAGNETIC FIELDS
* "WAITING FOR SUPERMAN"—THE FLAMING LIPS
* "TRUE LOVE WAITS"—RADIOHEAD
* "I HOPE YOU'RE HAPPY NOW"—ELVIS COSTELLO

## FALLING IN LOVE PLAYLIST

* "DROP AND ANCHOR"—MATES OF STATE
* "JANUARY WEDDING"—AVETT BROTHERS
* "IF YOU FALL"—AZURE RAY
* "ABSOLUTELY CUCKOO"—THE MAGNETIC FIELDS
* "FRIDAY I'M IN LOVE"—THE CURE
* "I'VE BEEN WAITING"—MATTHEW SWEET
* "THE LUCKIEST"—BEN FOLDS
* "FAMILY TREE"—BEN KWELLER
* "MAKE YOU FEEL MY LOVE"—ADELE
* "JUST LIKE HEAVEN"—THE CURE
* "HAPPINESS RUNS"—DONOVAN
* "THE WEATHER"—BUILT TO SPILL
* "LA LA LOVE YOU"—THE PIXIES
* "TO BE ALONE WITH YOU"—SUFJAN STEVENS
* "I'LL BE YOUR MIRROR"—THE VELVET UNDERGROUND
* "GREATEST YOU CAN FIND"—KEREN ANN
* "IF I THINK OF LOVE"—LISA GERMANO

So what finally snapped me out of it? He broke up with me. Yep. It was the first time I'd been broken up with since my early twenties, when a director I was dating flew across the country to film a movie and promptly started an affair with an actress he'd just met. "Do you want to break up with me?" I asked the director point-blank on the phone, after noticing how many times she popped up in our conversations. I think he was taken aback by my bluntness, but nevertheless, he hedged, Clinton style. "Um . . . I just feel like I am . . . *lost in the stars.*" I italicize his reply because that is the way it sounded to me at the time. It was just so inane and clichéd—like when someone tells a story and makes the quotation marks with their fingers. "Don't do that!" I want to scream. "You don't need the quotes if you're *telling* the story." I sat on the phone for what seemed like a long time and listened to the sound of the long distance between us. Then I sincerely thanked my wayward director for making the breakup a whole lot easier. Yes, my ego was slightly bruised at the time, but it perked up a few weeks later when the actress dumped him and ran off and married his lead actor in the film.

This time, all those years later, there were no laughable sad clichés to make things easier. I couldn't tell my friends that he was just a shallow jerk who wasn't worth my time. My heart was broken, and the worst part was I suddenly knew that I had no one to blame but myself. He had sadly, but calmly, told me that he understood why I wanted all of the things that I did, but he was afraid that he wouldn't be able to give them to me. I backpedaled and tried to downplay every demand that I had lobbed at him during the past few months. He wouldn't budge, having made up his mind. I was devastated. I remember riding in a taxi the next day and sobbing to my friend Victoria on the phone about how I had ruined everything.

"He loves you," she assured me. "I know he does."

"But how do you know?" I sputtered between racking sobs. "You think everyone (sob, sob) loves me, just because you do (sob, sob)." Sometimes when I talk to my friend Victoria, it is a bit like talking to my mother. She has very little objectivity when it comes to her friends, just as my mother, like most mothers, believes that everyone sees in her offspring what she does.

She talked me into driving straight to her apartment so that she could feed me and put me to bed—I had been up the whole night crying. I hung up and told the cabdriver (who happened to be Greek) the change in directions.

He peered at me in the rearview mirror with dark sympathetic eyes.

"You OK, miss?"

I wiped my face. "Yeah. It's just, my boyfriend just broke up with me . . . He's Greek!" I blurted out, before promptly bursting into tears again.

"Hellenas!" he shouted. "Does he love you?"

"He . . . he said he did," I sniffed.

"So he loves you. He says he loves you? He loves you." He shrugged his shoulders like it was the simplest thing in the world.

"I hope so," I said.

"Don't worry. He'll be back. Greek men don't fall out of love like that," he said, snapping his fingers.

"I hope you're right."

"I'm right. I know. I'm Greek. It's not over, I promise you." He banged on his steering wheel for emphasis. "I give him a week. Maybe less."

Somehow I found myself reassured by the cabbie's insistence. Even if I couldn't totally believe it, I was immensely comforted by the kindness of strangers. Especially in this case, when he was a Greek stranger with an "evil eye" dangling from the rearview mirror. I gave him an extra big tip, which he tried to refuse.

"*Efharisto*," I said thanking him with one of the few Greek words I knew.

"*Parakalo*," he replied. "Less than a week!" he called out through the window as he drove off beeping his horn at me.

As it happened, my cabbie was right. He did come back in less than a week, but in the meantime, I had done some soul-searching of my own and decided to snap out of it. I am not one for wallowing, at least not for an extended period of time. My pride won't let me do it. I decided that the only way I would be happy was to move on and let him go. It was a variation of the "If you love someone, set them free" theory of love (with thanks to Sting for indelibly planting this in our collective brains).

In our first conversations after getting back together, I promised not to bring up the *baby* word for at least two years. (I might have fudged that a little, but it was an honest pledge at the time.) He promised not to get overwhelmed by the onslaught of female emotion and to let me know when I started to freak him out. I in turn promised not to freak out when he freaked out. We went back and forth, batting promises to each other in an amorous equivalent of table tennis, and nine years and three kids later, we are still promising each other everything.

# ORIGINS

In the beginning
there was the word
typed out on a borrowed electric keyboard,
a pageantry of autobiography and flirtation,
anecdotes about pinecones, the aesthetics of fictitious brotherhood,
primitive royalty.

In the beginning
there was ice cream, plucked from the lowboy freezer
of a twenty-four-hour delicatessen on a forgotten Manhattan street corner
on an unforgettable night.

We should have been tired. Scared. Timid.
Instead we were wide awake and bold,
bumping against each other with all the oblivious,
willful glee of tectonic plates.
Mountain ranges rattled.
Buildings shook.
The chassis of the smallest cars suffered further indignities.

In the beginning
the future was as unfathomable as the spectral meddling fingers of God,
that is to say, wholly imaginary, brazenly unknown,

How much could have gone wrong.

Sometimes I amaze myself thinking about
the thousands of missteps that could have led us,
like blindfolded assistants crossing the knifethrower's stage,
right past each other.
It's so easy to miss our finest trajectory.
We could have been nothing more than
receding footfalls,
conjured up years after the performance has ended,

a flash of darkened curiosity.
My pulse flurries and furies at the thought.
We know so little.
Chemistry is a blur.
Geography is an embarrassment.
And I routinely forget the age of the Earth.
Even in retrospect our ignorance is tremendous.
So how, then, could we possibly have known
about each other?

Maybe there's more.
Under the skin
is the muscle
and under the muscle
is the bone,
and under the bone . . . what?

Thought?
Space?
Intention?

Tell me where music comes from
and I will tell you what love is.

Every song contains within it
the expanding and great-hearted enormity
of the universe, a phenomenon that quietly mirrors
in its complexity
in its beauty
in its grace
and in my gratitude

the outrageous splendor of your love.

—PANIO GIANOPOULOS
JULY 6, 2008

Chapter Six

# NEVER WEAR
# SANDALS IN
# THE KITCHEN

A FRENCHMAN ONCE MUSED TO ME PHILOSOPHICALLY,
"IT IS HARD FOR ZEE WOMAN TO HAVE A GOOD RELA-
TIONSHIP WITH HER ASS, SINCE IT IS ALWAYS BEHIND
HER." Not to say that I don't care about my ass. I do. Marginally. Prob-
ably not as much as some people do. But then I get a grip and remember
my priorities, and for this I turn to French*women* rather than men.

There is a quote, often attributed to the great style icon Catherine
Deneuve, that goes something like: "At a certain age, you must choose
between your face and your ass." Given the fact that Ms. Deneuve is a
classic Parisian, the Mecca of Michelin-rated cuisine, how could she not
choose the former? When I moved to Paris, I made the same choice—I
didn't even have to wait for my forties. I was pretty clear in my twenties what mattered to me. When I die, I don't intend to have it written
on my grave "She was skinny." I would much prefer "She mastered the
soufflé" or "Her hollandaise never separated."

I have always been interested in food. My own mother is a chef and compulsive cookbook collector. The first French words I learned were *bon appétit*, which is how my mother signed cookbooks that she gave me as a child. This is because her idol, Julia Child, signed her autographs this way. I grew up with a mother who cooked everything from scratch. Mostly this was for budgetary reasons, but I also think that she developed a great sense of pride from what she could create in the kitchen. The house always smelled of baking bread. We never went to school with store-bought bread, so of course for a short time during our adolescence, we were convinced that we were missing something. My sister, Beth, once wailed to my mother in the supermarket bread aisle, "You don't love me. You don't *want* me to grow twelve different ways," referring to the Wonder bread slogan of the time.

My siblings and I would stare longingly at our friends' Wonder bread bologna sandwiches at school. Miraculously, we found that our friends were always more than willing to make a trade for our fluffy sandwiches with homemade bread and fresh preserves.

Even now, there is no scent that I find more comforting than the smell of bread baking. For this reason, the whole Atkins fad just passed me by. How could I give up something that I loved so much? It isn't just the fact that bread tastes delicious. It's also one of my most basic and fondest childhood memories. A good friend of mine who came from a troubled home spent many days at my family's home. She said that just walking into my home and smelling the freshly baked bread filled her with a sense of well-being, that there was someplace she could go to where everything was right in the world.

The most remarkable part is that my mother didn't even know how to cook when she first got married, a skill that was pretty much a prerequisite to matrimony when my parents met in the late fifties. Apparently the very first meal that she attempted—which wasn't really a meal at all—was sticky buns. It was such a success that my father was convinced that someone else had made them. He kept trying to get her to "fess up," but she insisted that it was she who had created the delicacy. It was the beginning of my mother's long love affair with food and then subsequently, and through association, mine.

The first time I visited Paris I was thirteen years old. At that time I was under the misconception that everything you ate there was a culinary masterpiece. I thought that you could drink wine from a tap and it would be ambrosia. Admittedly, my palate wasn't as refined as it is today—having lived there for a good length of time later in life, I am able to confidently state that it is just as easy to have a bad meal in Paris as it is anywhere else in the world. But the good ones are incomparable.

Whenever anyone finds out that I lived in France, I always get the same question. What were you doing there? The answer: eating incredible food and learning French . . . so I could keep on eating more incredible food. I think I always suspected that food could taste like that, but to live in a city where on any given night you could go out and eat something as simple as *steak frites* with a *tarte tatin* for dessert and feel like it was the most delicious thing you'd ever eaten never lost its novelty. And the most amazing thing? I never gained weight. The only time that I put on a few pounds was, surprise, surprise, when I returned to the United States for visits. I'm pretty sure that the reason for this is the quality of the ingredients there and the lack of processed foods.

# THE FIVE BIGGEST MISTAKES HOME COOKS MAKE

Let's admit it, cooking can be a daunting prospect. But it's also hugely rewarding—and there's no better time than now. What with the proliferation of farmers' markets and the slow food revolution, not to mention the seemingly endless recession, if you've ever had any interest in cooking at home, here's your chance. Not all of us have the time to drop it all and go to chef's training, of course, so I've asked my friend Taite Pearson, a longtime professional chef, for some behind-the-scenes tips and tricks for beginners.

### MISTAKE 1: FEAR OF EXPERIMENTATION

Many people say "I can't cook" or "I only know how to make . . . blah blah blah." Cooking is an adventure. Be brave. Use ingredients you have never used before. It is likely that even your mistakes will bring you joy in the kitchen and pleasure at the table. A phrase I always try to keep in mind when cooking is "Good judgment comes from experience, and experience comes from bad judgment" (Barry LePatner).

## MISTAKE 2: INFERIOR INGREDIENTS

When purchasing groceries, buy the best possible quality product you can afford. Buy seasonally correct and local whenever possible. Visit the farmers' markets. The better-tasting the ingredients you start with, the better-tasting the final dish will be. What we buy and how we approach it affects those we nurture and the environment, and it just plain feels good to know where our ingredients came from.

## MISTAKE 3: POOR STORAGE

Research and understand the proper way to store your foodstuffs. This will keep them at the highest quality until they are used, avoid contamination, and lengthen the life of pantry goods.

## MISTAKE 4: SKIMPING ON EQUIPMENT

Every home cook doesn't need a kitchen full of fancy gadgets, but the equipment we use will make cooking more enjoyable. Again, buy the best quality you can. All you need are a couple of really good quality pans (one sauté, one sauce), a great chef's knife that feels good in your hands, and a paring knife. Add tools as you go and as your repertoire broadens. Splurge on something every once in a while. It will encourage you to spend more time in the kitchen.

## MISTAKE 5: EXCLUDING CHILDREN

Include them in the whole process. Enrich their lives with food. They are the future.

In Paris, nothing is fast. When I first moved there, in my twenties, I used to go around to the cafés and try to order coffee "to go." The café owners were always perplexed by this—the very idea of coffee "to go" mystified them. Why would anyone want to take their coffee with them, guzzling it midstride, when they could sit at a table instead and enjoy it at their leisure, while engaged in conversation with friends? They never had a proper cup, so I usually received the coffee in a little plastic cup unintended for hot beverages. And the amount of coffee in the cup was so minuscule that it hardly seemed worth the effort. They don't drink their coffee in huge, oversize cups with Italian names. It was soon explained to me that in France the act of drinking coffee is a social thing. Enough time to share a few gossipy tidbits with your friends and maybe a cigarette (when everyone was still smoking in cafés) before heading off to wherever you are going. The French don't like to multitask the way Americans are expected to. In time I stopped trying to take my coffee away with me. In truth, there was really no reason to. I had all the time in the world, so I used it. I started a morning ritual of ordering my coffee. *Un double express avec un nuage de lait.* And a *croissant—ordinaire, s'il vous plaît.* Ordering a croissant *ordinaire* means that you order it without the extra butter. You can tell the difference by the shape. *Croissant beurre* is shaped, well, like a crescent. *Ordinaire* is shaped like a fluffy crab, the tips curled toward each other. My morning indulgence was *une orange pressée—une double.* Which was really just a glass of fresh-squeezed orange juice filled to the top of the glass. Otherwise, the café owner would fill the glass halfway with juice and deliver it with a pitcher of water and a bowl of sugar. Having a full glass of orange juice was an American habit I deliberately never lost, even though it was ridiculously expensive, costing nearly ten U.S. dollars. My French friends would stare at me as I gulped down my orange juice in the morning like some greedy emperor. If I really felt like shocking them, I would order another.

"She ees so American," they would remark. "Eet ees because she ees from Californie, *sans doute.*"

## BREAD

France is the Mecca of all Meccas for bread lovers. The crusty baguette, with cheese and sliced ham, became a standby for me. In fact, I think the week I first moved to Paris, I ate ham and cheese sandwiches every day.

Of course at the time I didn't know that I had moved there yet. Initially, I went there for a film. I finagled it into my contract to fly my friend Julia there with me and we installed ourselves in the Palais Royal (home to the writer Colette, among other luminaries), expecting to return to the United States at the end of the summer. But in the back of my mind, I suspect there was some hint of what was to come. Before leaving Los Angeles, I had put my house up for sale, moved everything into storage, and then carted seven large suitcases with me to Paris. My unconscious clearly had plans of its own.

After a while—and hundreds of baguettes—I started to notice a sign that was posted in dozens of French cafés. LE PAIN POILÂNE EST SERVI ICI. What is this *Pain Poilâne* and why is it so special that they want to advertise it everywhere? I wondered. Upon investigation, I learned that it is a sourdough country bread, made with stone ground flour, natural fermentation, and baked in a wood-burning oven. It has a slightly tart, but earthy, mineral-y flavor. The loaf is big and oblong, about four and a half pounds, and you can slice the bread in unusually big slices. It also has another advantage: it lasts for days, unlike the classic baguettes, which get rock hard after one day. Soon I started making the trek to the Poilâne bakery on the Rue de Cherche-Midi in St.-Germain-des-Prés to pick up my own *Pain Poilâne* and a little apple tart in puff pastry.

One year, my mother came to visit me for New Year's Eve. It was an exceptionally cold winter in Paris at the time. And somehow, cold in Paris just seems colder. Maybe it is the icy wet air traveling up from the

Seine, or the big stone buildings, but it was dismally cold—the kind of cold that gives you a chill when you step outside to pick up the paper, a chill you can't lose for the rest of the day. Since my mother was in town, I felt the need to show her around, show her all the places that I loved, all of the reasons I had chosen to move there. We walked around most of the afternoon until our feet were frozen, and then right before we headed back to my apartment in the Marais, we made a little detour to the Pain Poilâne bakery. As usual, there was a line outside of people waiting to get in. I hopped from foot to foot, shivering.

"Mom, the line is too long! Let's come back another time."

"Let me just look in the window a second," my mother said, walking up to the glass and peering in at the various, beautiful loaves. She is a professionally trained chef, but her true passion has always been baking.

Just then a hired car pulled up and a man in a long cashmere coat stepped out with a little girl. They strode into the bakery as if they owned the place.

"Will you look at these, Molly?" my mother said as she pointed to one of the loaves on display.

A few seconds later, the man suddenly reappeared and asked my mother if we would like to tour the bakery. The man was Lionel Poilâne, and yes—he actually did own the place! My mother and I blinked at each other, completely surprised. Yes, of course we would! Poilâne took us downstairs to where the ovens were located. The room was as hot as a furnace. Three shirtless young men fed the famous loaves into the oven. My mom marveled at the oven. (I marveled at the men.) Monsieur Poilâne showed us around the rest of the bakery, and at our departure gave us a gift of some apple tarts. I never knew what made him invite us in, the reason for his generosity. All he said, by way of a reason, was that he could see that my mother was American, and that she was truly interested in the bread. He said that he wanted to send her home with a *bon souvenir*, which in French means a fond memory. And he did. It was the undisputed highlight of her trip. Not too long afterward, I read in the paper that Lionel Poilâne died in a helicopter crash along with his wife. The little girl that I saw that day now runs the entire Poilâne enterprise. I've always wanted to thank her father, for his bread, and for the *bon souvenir*.

## CHEESE

Never cut the nose of the cheese! I learned this the hard way one Sunday afternoon in the French countryside. Every weekend my boyfriend and I would make the trek to the outskirts of Paris to have Sunday lunch with the family—come rain or come shine. These lunches, though invariably delicious, were also a bit uncomfortable for me. I found my high school French to be sorely lacking, and though most of the family attempted to speak slowly, or occasionally to converse in English for me, the meals were usually conducted in rapid-fire French, full of overlapping enthusiasm and in jokes. "In my country, I speak French," his seventeen-year-old sister sniffed. I spent most of the time trying to follow the conversations, and then when my head started to hurt, I'd just kind of space out and have conversations with myself. My favorite part of the meal was inevitably the cheese plate (always served at the end of the meal, either in place of or accompanying dessert). Having grown up in America, where the most exotic kind of cheese was Roquefort, the different kinds of cheeses on the average Sunday lunch cheese plate were always a treat. The fresh and nutty Reblochon (its name, incidentally, comes from the verb *reblocher,* which means "to pinch a cow's udder again"), a creamy Camembert, a tangy *chèvre.* I reached across the table to serve myself a slice of Saint-Nectaire when I became aware of a sudden, strange lull in conversation. And then a cacophony of French voices erupted.

"*Le nez!*"

"*Le nez!*"

"*Pas le nez!*"

I pulled my hand back as if I were about to be scorched and looked at my boyfriend for an explanation. He explained to me how one never cuts the nose of the cheese. It is considered the pinnacle of rudeness. It's funny how the French decide what is rude and what is not. I endured countless dinner parties where the main topic of conversation was how backward America was, how insincere and poorly educated we are, how Americans only care about money, how they smile far too much ("What are you Americans hiding that you need to smile so much?"). I even sat through a party once while a drunken Frenchman tried to convince me that most American women have fat calves.

"What?" I yelled over "Is This Love" by Bob Marley. Incidentally, the French love their Bob Marley every bit as much as their Western keg party counterparts. I was sure that I had misunderstood him. "American women have fat *what?*"

"*Les mollets,*" he said as he lunged for mine to give them a drunken squeeze. I swatted him away.

"Thanks for letting me know." I considered pointing out something

to him about Frenchmen and their noses. Maybe by asking him if he could smoke in the shower with his honker, but then I decided it would take too long for me to translate. I still was at that frustrating, just-on-the-edge-of-fluency level, the point where I could order everything perfectly in a restaurant, easily buy my groceries, but when it came to humor, I was infuriatingly slow and clumsy. It is very difficult to be funny in another language. Or, at least, funny when you mean to be. It is astonishingly easy to be funny when you don't mean to be. And the truth of the matter is that I happen to have a fondness for big noses, I secretly feared that I have fat calves, but mostly, I don't particularly like being rude.

Back at Sunday lunch, my boyfriend's family had now launched into a sort of ditty that reminded me of when I was eight years old and staying at my cousin's house, where they had a very elaborate song about not putting elbows on the table. The reason never to cut the nose off the cheese—according to the song—goes something like this: If you always cut the tip off, eventually the last person who decides they want to sample the cheese will get only the rind. *"Mon Dieu!"* But if you always cut it on the angle, everyone will have just the right proportion of cheese and rind, and everyone is happy. This is a lesson that I will never forget, thanks to my day of Sunday lunch humiliation— one of many. There was also the day of never pouring the wine while holding it by the neck, but that's another story. If you learn anything from my book at all, just remember: nose, neck, and elbows. You'll be fine.

## MY FRIEND MARIE'S THOUGHTS ON DINNER PARTIES

FLOWERS THAT TELL THE SEASON

CANDLES, SIMPLE

BEAUTIFUL LINEN, USED SPARINGLY

PEOPLE WHO ENJOY BEING PLEASED

IMPECCABLE FOOD, EVEN IF IT IS CHEESE OR BREAD

AN EXTRAVAGANCE IN SOMETHING, BUT NOT EVERYTHING

THE IDEA OF CREATING A PERFECT SETTING, OR SERIES OF MOMENTS, FOR SOMETHING THAT WILL PASS IN A COUPLE OF HOURS

# L'ASSIETTE DE FROMAGE (THE CHEESE PLATE)

It is easy to feel intimidated by the cheese plate. Especially when you are born in a country where "American cheese" isn't really cheese at all, but rather a highly processed cheeselike product. Learning about all of the different kinds of cheeses can be a daunting but exciting venture. Now, more than ever, we have a vast selection of cheeses to choose from that come not just from other countries but also from artisanal producers in the United States.

To put together a simple but solid selection, aim for a four-cheese plate, about one ounce apiece, that progresses from mildest to strongest. I prefer to start with a fresh goat cheese, such as a Selles-sur-Cher or Valencay. Some people like to have a triple crème, or a Brie or Camembert, but if your taste tends to veer toward the stronger, you can begin with a Taleggio or Epoisses. Despite the vehemence of my French friends who tried to convince me that cheddar was not a *real* cheese, I do not agree. Any cheese plate of mine must include a real English cheddar. Next is either a genuine aged Gouda or the incredible Roomano (not Romano), both Dutch. These aren't that easy to find, especially in good condition, but they're incredible. And, finally, a blue cheese—Roquefort, Stilton, or Gorgonzola.

As for wine pairings: ideally each cheese gets its own little glass, but in reality, it's not really necessary. Whatever red is left on the table is good for the stinky cheeses and the cheddar, but the Dutch cheese and blue would be better off with a little dessert wine like a muscat/moscato or Sauternes, or even something fortified like port or sherry.

A baguette or a Poilâne-like peasant bread should be on the table, but not on the plate itself! It's also nice to have some fruit on the side—figs, grapes, or dried apricots—and with fresh goat and other really mild cheeses I also like to serve either a fruit jam or apricot/quince paste and maybe a nice aged balsamic vinegar.

Most important, as my fellow foodie and turophile* Chris insists, the cheeses must come from a good cheese shop. Most supermarkets just don't have genuine cheeses. Even if the label claims ENGLISH FARMHOUSE CHEDDAR and it costs twenty dollars a pound, it's still most likely not the real thing (and in flavor and texture, the fake doesn't come close). All those great names—cheddar, Gouda, Gruyère, etc.—were bastardized into awful things precisely because the originals are such fantastic artifacts, well worth finding.

*Turophile: Pronunciation: \ˈtu̇-ə-fi(-ə)l,ˈtyu̇r-\
Function: noun
Etymology: irregular from Greek tyros cheese +
English -phile —: a connoisseur of cheese : a cheese fancier

## WINE

And to finish off the trifecta: wine! The holy trinity. Bread, cheese, and wine. I think I could live on these three things alone. In fact, at times I have.

Until I moved to France, I didn't know much about wine. All I basically knew was overly oaky Chardonnay (which I confess, I used to like, and now can't stand). As for red wine, I rarely ever drank it, mostly because I didn't know anything about it. Then I met a Frenchman from Bordeaux, and everything changed. I learned the years that were the best ('82, '89), I visited the vineyards (St. Émilion, Médoc, Pauillac), I became a veritable wine snob. My poor family had to endure me on holidays, turning up my nose when they would open a perfectly decent bottle of Cabernet. *"Vin de soif,"* I would say, which roughly translates as "A decent table wine." Or if I was feeling less charitable, I'd huff, *"Jus de chausette,"* which means, "Juice from the socks." They say that babies are particularly cute and cuddly so that their parents will love and nurture them. But what keeps parents loving their children after they grow up and move to France? Habit?

Soon after I moved to Paris, I spent a ridiculous amount of money on what is arguably the best bottle of wine that exists in the world, Le Petrus, in what is considered to be one of the best years in recent history, 1989. My apartment in the Marais actually had a *cave*, which lent itself to even more feverish collecting. My Bordelais boyfriend encouraged my enthusiasm, and together we went on a frenzied wine-purchasing binge, and he kept track of them on a computer spreadsheet—the only thing that he was seriously organized about. A couple of years later, my *cave* was robbed. The French thieves chose to forgo the spare VCR, the racks of clothing, the skis; in fact the only thing they seemed to be interested in was the wine. Three cases were stolen. Mercifully, without the spreadsheet, they missed the Petrus and a few other choice bottles. I breathed a sigh of relief. What luck! My nectar of the gods was safe. Then a few years after that, I lost all my wine, every last bottle, in my divorce from the French boyfriend whom I eventually married.

I drink Italian wine now.

On a lark, one spring I decided to go to culinary school in Paris. I figured if I was ever going to do something like that, France was the place to do it. I researched various options online and finally decided on the Ritz Escoffier school. I already had a fondness for the Ritz, since I had joined the gym there. Unlike the United States, where there seems to be a gym on every corner—next to the nail salon and pharmacy—gyms are not very easy to come by in Europe. An actor whom I had met at a French film festival persuaded me that the best (if not only) place to work out was the Ritz. It didn't take a lot of convincing. I enthusiastically joined the gym and went three times a week. I jogged on the treadmill next to Gregory Peck, swam in the mosaic swimming pool while the philosopher Bernard-Henri Lévy tapped away on his portable computer poolside. It was obscenely luxurious, and I loved it.

On my first day of cooking school, I dressed carefully in the provided uniform. (I have always loved uniforms. Some days I actually miss not being able to dress in my high school uniform.) My cooking school uniform was almost identical to the uniform that my mom wore when she attended culinary school years before: checkered pants, white jacket (with RITZ ESCOFFIER stitched in elaborate blue script), and a jaunty white cap. Since the weather was fairly warm outside, I decided to complete the outfit by wearing my favorite sandals.

When I arrived at the school, the chef immediately narrowed his eyes, and with a long skinny paring knife he pointed to my bare toes sticking out of the sandals. He informed me that I was never to wear

them again, and if I had been taking the course for a grade, I would have failed on the spot. I gulped. *"Oui, Chef."* I got my own back a few days later, however, when he stuck his finger into where I was filleting a giant cod.

Entitled "The Taste of Provence," the course ran for a week. During that time, we prepared *Pissaldiere, soupe de pistou Rouget,* the perfect *aoli,* "*Zee Rolls-Royce of bouillabaisse*" (as our chef referred to his method of preparing the famous peasant fisherman's soup, minus any of what a peasant would have actually put in it). It was a hectic, exciting, challenging time, and while I remember very little of what I learned, I'll never forget the sheer joy I felt during that week—and joy is as important to me as knowing how to expertly debone a chicken.

The translator that the Ritz had hired for the class spoke only basic English, so I ended up as the de facto translator. It was a great personal victory, tantamount to being able to cuss out a French café waiter with authority. (This takes a minimum of two years—at least it did on my part.) I was happy to be of some service to my fellow foodies, and to be able to feel like a teacher's pet. By this point, Chef had forgiven me for nearly slicing his finger off. In fact I think he found me somewhat useful (at least linguistically, certainly not for my culinary acumen). He would rattle off a long and involved explanation and then turn to me and bark, "Translate!" which I dutifully did.

Every evening, before leaving, the class would sit at a long communal table and eat what we had prepared during the day. After a couple of glasses of carefully selected wine, our chef would loosen up and chat pleasantly with the students. I grilled him about his favorite restaurants in Paris. How did he judge the merits of a restaurant? Was it the lightness of the sauce? The inventiveness of the combination of ingredients? His answer surprised me. The perfectly dressed green salad.

A green salad is the hardest to get right, he explained. It's always over- or underdressed, usually over—like a starlet at an Oscar party.

He told me that recently he had been to a restaurant in the 16th Arrondissement and ordered what turned out to be the perfect green salad. He thought it was a fluke, he had never tasted one so perfect, so he ordered another. Same thing. "If you can get zee salad right, everything else, *c'est simple*." He then did the typical French thing of putting his lips together and blowing out dismissively. After a couple glasses of wine myself, I started to develop a pretty good crush on him. I let myself imagine what it would be like to have a boyfriend who was a chef. He would definitely help me master the hollandaise. We would open a restaurant together. I would be a charming hostess, he would be the surly genius in back. It was either the wine talking, or the chef's uniform, because a few days later I saw him at a fellow classmate's cocktail party, dressed in a leather biker's jacket and jeans about two sizes too tight. The effect was devastating. My crush collapsed like a beginner's soufflé.

# BOUILLABAISSE RECIPE

I thought that nothing could compare to the bouillabaisse recipe that I learned while at Ritz Escoffier in Paris. Then I moved to New York and befriended a beautiful ex–opera singer/garden designer and mad chef Marie Viljoen. It could be her company, or her tiny charming Brooklyn apartment (that she blogs extensively about in "66 Square Feet"— which are exactly the dimensions of her terrace garden). Mostly I think it's her dedication to getting it right and not caring about how long it takes. This is definitely a dish that is all about the preparation! Here is Marie's master recipe in her own words:

This is not an authentic bouillabaisse. There may not be one authentic bouillabaisse, but this is authentically mine. If you have a free day you can make this in one day, or half, since you must buy the fish the same day. If not, make the stock ahead and freeze or start again the next day.

*serves 6*

One each of three different kinds of fish, with heads, bones, etc., cleaned, scaled, and roughly chopped (for example, snapper, John Dory, rouget, branzino). You can fillet these fish and save the fillets for adding to the soup later, but then you must make the whole thing the same day.

1½ lbs of shrimp, with shells and, preferably, heads. Shell and clean the shrimp, keep tails for soup, and reserve shells for stock.

A lobster if you are rich, two if you know a diver. Reserve tail meat and keep the chopped body and head. No, the green stuff isn't icky, it's good. It's the tomalley. Liver, OK? Keep it. Throw away the gritty sac though (you can't be squeamish). Also the dead man's fingers (lungs, blegh . . . OK, a little squeamish).

3 large onions, chopped finely

1 head (not clove, head) of garlic, chopped finely

2 bulbs fennel, chopped finely

6 tomatoes, skinned, chopped, not finely

2 tbsp tomato paste

2 bottles of good white wine, not wooded, slightly fruity, but dry. It has got to be wine you would drink (and would be very nice if it *is* the wine you will drink . . .)

3 bay leaves

3 sprigs thyme

1 bunch parsley

10 peppercorns

1 tbsp sugar

salt

## HOW TO MAKE THE STOCK (OR "SOUL" OF THE SOUP)

Pour a healthy splash of olive oil into a large pot. Add onions, then garlic, sauté for about five minutes on medium to low heat, till translucent. Increase heat to at least medium and add fennel and cook another five minutes. Stir not to burn. Add chopped fish heads and bones, and prawn and lobster shells. Stir everything nicely so they're all in contact with the heat. Add tomatoes and tomato paste, stir again. Add herbs and peppercorns and sugar. Toss in two bottles of wine or until everything is covered. Add water if necessary. It will probably be necessary. Bring to a boil and reduce so that it's simmering (lots of steam, surface barely shaking), and skim off any scum that rises. Clean the kitchen.

The stock should cook for about an hour. Taste it at this time and add salt. Through a sieve, pour all the stock into a big bowl. You'll have to do this in batches, as the sieve fills up with bits. Push all these bits very hard against the mesh to get every little drop out. In my extreme moments I have put bits into a blender. I also broke the blender—but the idea is to get every ounce of goodness out of the bits.

OK—now you have a bowlful of stock. At this point I commit *another* heresy. I reduce it. Just by about a fifth. Which means you put it back into the big, now-clean pot, back on high heat and bring it to a boil, then reduce to a serious simmer, and let it do that for about thirty-five minutes.

There is an *alternative*, and since I'm going to hell already, I can tell you. It's . . . *chicken stock*. Real is best . . . but a *c-c-c-cube* does wonders. Phew, I feel unburdened. I would say I have done it 33.3 percent of the time when for some reason the stock just doesn't taste right.

## FOR THE FINISHED BOUILLABAISSE

Add a large of pinch saffron. Add fillets from two or preferably three kinds of white fish, like the fish mentioned on page 156. They must be sliced into nice but not uniform bits. Bear in mind that the biggest pieces will take longest to cook and will be added a little earlier than the small pieces. Personally, I like the skin off. Boiled fish skin. Brrrr.

Add prawns or shrimp, either in the shell, cleaned; or the naked bodies; or entire, with head (this last will add an additional deliciousness to the soup, if you go for it). The quantity is worked out by estimating how many prawns or shrimp each person may like to eat. If you splurge and buy langoustes, get one each, tiger prawns, one or two each, etc.

If you are having lobster, add the tail meat and claw meat if you live where lobsters have claws. For the superdeluxe version, add Dungeness crab claws and VERY fresh lump crabmeat. Add cockles or very little clams, about 1½ pounds, de-sanded by soaking in fresh water for ten minutes.

Add mussels, same and de-bearded, and only if you have a super-reliable fish person or local tidal rock. Mussels have made me very sick more than once (but never from my own bouillabaisse!).

Now before you start the final stage, some helpful hints:

Make sure you have invited people *you really like* to dinner. If you have things with shells that need to be cracked, buy claw crackers. If you don't have claw crackers, don't have things with shells. Have very big napkins, preferably of the pretty dishcloth variety. They will get stained. Have very good bread. Make it into toasts. Have aioli, or better, rouille.

So you have stock. You have beautiful fish. Everything else is ready. Your wine is chilling, there's a green salad for later, or before if you must, and poached pears or roasted peaches, depending on your season, for dessert.

Bring your stock to a simmer. Add your large pinch of saffron. First add the pieces of fish that look the biggest. Then the small guys. Add the cockles and mussels last* (as you're doing this, increase the heat, because the cold fish will take heat out of the pot and slow everything down). When these shellfish have opened, it's ready. Throw out any you see that stay closed.

Serve in wide bowls, giving everyone a bit of everything. Dunk bread. Slather rouille or aoili (sometimes I stir some in—yet more heresy, before serving) on the bread. Drink icy white wine. Be very happy to be eating this with people you like.

---

* *If you have small prawns or lobster tail, cut into pieces and add these last—it is sinful to overcook them.*

## THE PERFECT DINNER PARTY

I love dinner parties more than any other kind of party. I love going to them, and I love giving them. I don't think there is any steadfast rule about the right way to give a party, although there are a few guidelines that I have gleaned from experience.

### 1. MAKE SURE THAT YOUR GUESTS CAN EAT WHAT YOU PREPARE.

It's always a good idea to find out if there are any vegetarians. Or even just picky eaters. I once sent out an e-mail a couple of days before a dinner I was hosting and received a litany of likes and dislikes from a new friend. If I hadn't known that she was talking about herself, I would have thought that she was listing her son's allergies. But as annoying as this is, it is far better than having a guest pick the offending vegetable out of the sauce.

### 2. PREPARE EVERYTHING THAT YOU CAN THE NIGHT BEFORE.

This may seem obvious—many cookbooks recommend it— but I never realized how much smoother everything goes until I actually tried it. It works particularly well with soups or stews. Anything that has a million little things that need to be chopped up and simmered for hours. In fact, at the risk of sounding like my Greek father-in-law, it actually *is* better the next day.

3. **ALLOW ENOUGH TIME TO GET YOURSELF TOGETHER BEFORE YOUR GUESTS ARRIVE.**

   Not to say that everything has to be finished and served immediately—there is something nice about hanging out in the kitchen while the chef puts the finishing touches on the meal.

4. **POLITELY DECLINE WHEN ASKED "IS THERE ANYTHING I CAN DO TO HELP?"**

   They are just being polite. The last thing your guests should have to do is be put to work when they arrive. Unless, that is, you observe a look of terror in their eyes at having to socialize with anyone. If that is the case, throw an apron on them and find something easy for them to do.

5. **CHOOSE YOUR SOUND TRACK WISELY.**

   I feel that every party should have its own soundtrack. It shouldn't be loud enough to overpower the conversation, but as a general rule, classical should be reserved for brunch. Jazz is my personal favorite— though having grown up listening to twenties jazz music, it is my musical equivalent to comfort food. It gives the evening a sort of vintage Woody Allen–movie flair and somehow makes people sound smarter.

6. **KEEP THE MEAL SIMPLE.**

   Contrary to what a lot of people seem to think, simpler is better when it comes to the actual dinner. Most people are just thankful not to have to eat out yet again or be at home thawing out whatever they have in their freezer. They are downright grateful to eat anything warm and tasty put before them, no matter how simple. So if you aren't used to cooking for a bunch of adults, best to keep your stress level down and stick with something relatively easy. A roasted chicken is one of the easiest, and conversely impressive, dishes. It is my standby. Accompanied by a green salad (perfectly dressed, of course), roasted potatoes, and French green beans. Roasted chicken is versatile too, in that it is one of those year-round meals. In spring and summer, you can serve it with a crisp Sauvignon Blanc, in fall and winter, switch to Poule au Pot and a Côte de Rhône.

## 7. BAG THE BUFFET.

This is a rule that I made up when I was still living with my parents as a teenager. My mother announced over Thanksgiving one year that the meal would be served "buffet style." I howled in protest. Buffet style? What are we, a cafeteria? To me, dinner is a time for everyone to sit together and pass things around. "Can you pass the bread?" is such a convivial phrase. The passing and the sharing. Buffets seem to take that away. If the reason for instituting a buffet is that there is just too much food to fit on one table, then you are probably serving too much food.

## 8. SIZE IT RIGHT.

I think the perfect number for a dinner party is six. Fewer than six can feel like a double date, more than six runs the risk of having two separate parties in one. It's nice to have different conversations going, but at some point they ought to converge, like the moment in a symphony when all of the leitmotifs come together. As a hostess, make sure that you draw out the shyer people and keep the conversation hogs in check. There are some differing opinions as to whether or not you need to separate couples. The classicists say absolutely, but the more progressive hostess in me says let people sit where they want. A night out should be enjoyable for everyone, and if that means sitting with your beloved, then that's where you should sit. In my case, having a night out with my husband, with our busy schedules and parenting responsibilities, seems like a treat. The last thing I want is to be shunted three seats away from him in the name of dinner party protocol. The one exception, however, is if you are the one throwing the party. In that case, I think it is a good idea to split the table. You cover half while your mate covers the other. That way you have the best chance of ensuring your guests are well taken care of.

## 9. DON'T WORRY ABOUT EVERYTHING MATCHING PERFECTLY.

It's charming if things are a little mismatched. It makes everything look less intentional, less precious. The wonderful thing about being invited into someone's home is just that: it is someone's *home*. It shouldn't feel like a film set or a magazine shoot. Tiny chips in the porcelain are fine, they won't bother anyone. I like little imperfections. And if a chipped saucer mortally offends someone, then ask yourself, do you really want such a stick-in-the-mud in your home?

## 10. MAKE SURE THAT YOU HAVE ENOUGH WINE TO LAST.

There is nothing more depressing than going to a dinner party and finding that the wine is gone. It is a surefire way to ensure that your guests are gone too. In fact, discreetly putting an end to the wine is the dinner party hostess's subtle way of letting you know it's time to hit the road, comparable to a restaurant's (not-so-subtle) habit of turning up the lights.

# WHAT TO BRING AS A HOSTESS GIFT

**DESSERT:** This is an easy way to win your hostess's heart. It's very common for the home cook to spend so much time concentrating on the entrée and appetizer and overall setup that the dessert gets neglected. Don't feel that this requires a major time commitment; sure, you can spend hours in your kitchen crafting the perfect profiteroles, but you can also opt for a basket of fresh strawberries from the market. Whatever you bring, err on the side of generous.

**CHAMPAGNE:** A lot of people think of champagne as an aperitif, but there is something really lovely about having a great bottle of champagne with dessert.

**FRESH HERBS:** No hostess will ever turn her nose up at flowers, but as an alternative, consider bringing clippings of fresh herbs. They don't have to be relevant to that evening's meal.

**PINEAPPLE:** A friend of mine has endeared himself to me forever by bringing over a pineapple one evening. It's that perfect combination of thought and whimsy.

# THE HONORED GUEST

One spring Marie and I were in a festive mood. The tulips had all come up on my rooftop terrace, and the weather was perfect. There was a climbing rose, Cecile Brunner, that had just come into bloom. I didn't know when I had planted this particular flower; though charming and fragrant when in bloom, it blooms for only a very short period of time, and then not again till the following year. It seemed like as good a reason as any to throw a party.

We invited our guests to the party in honor of the Cecile Brunner flower and concocted a special cocktail to go along with it: champagne with a coulis of raspberries.

Dining alfresco whenever possible is my motto. Especially in a city where we spend so much of the day cooped up indoors. The rooftop deck was the main reason I had chosen my apartment in Manhattan. Who needs a country house when you can dine among Japanese maples while gazing at the Chrysler building? Some of my fondest moments have been spent on the roof, either dining with friends, or during the day, working in the roof garden, my hands deep in the soft, warm dirt.

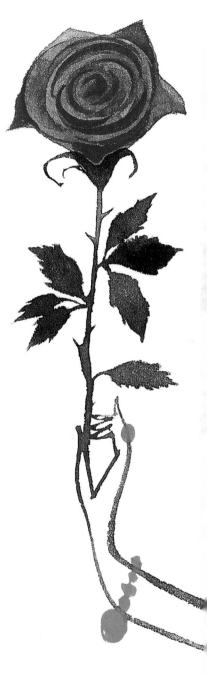

．．．．．．．．

Food is one of the true great pleasures of life, and I feel that it has been demonized to the point where so many people can't enjoy a perfectly healthy meal without having shame attached to it. I truly believe that this has led us down a disastrous road of modifying the way we eat to the point of not actually eating real food at all. I subscribe wholeheartedly to the Michael Pollan manifesto that he writes in his book *In Defense of Food*: "Eat food. Not too much. Mostly plants." And when he says food, he means *real food*, not edible foodlike substances, which is what we find all over the place in supermarkets today. The more we can get back in touch with real food, the healthier we, and our families, will be. And if you have the space, plant a little garden. Live off the fat of the land! I'm not saying that you need to dress like a pioneer and start churning your own butter, but planting your own small organic garden is a wonderful way to know what it is you are feeding yourself, and at the same time make food less abstract for your children. Kids tend to be far less suspicious of food and more willing to try it if they have some idea of where it came from.

Tending a garden also has the added benefit of being incredibly meditative for me—it's the part of the day when I don't have to talk, or answer, or even think. And the satisfaction of eating what you grow never ceases to be magical. I remember being a seventh grader and growing radishes in horticulture class. I was just as bored and blasé as all of my fellow students, but the day that we harvested and I got to take home a giant heap of radishes in a brown paper bag was thrilling. My family ate radishes for a week as I vigilantly checked to make sure that my hard-earned booty was being properly consumed. To this day I have a special fondness for radishes that goes far beyond their actual merit.

I realize that not everyone has the space for a full-blown garden, but it actually takes less space than you think. And a lot of vegetables can grow vertically (tomatoes, green beans), meaning that you can just throw them in an old wine barrel packed with soil. If you don't have room for even that, however, there is the option of finding a local community garden, something that is becoming more and more prevalent lately. It seems that it has finally dawned on us that we need to get out of processed food purgatory and back to our earth somehow.

# TRICKS THAT MODERN COOKS HAVE FORGOTTEN. . . OR PERHAPS NEVER LEARNED

My mom enrolled in chef's training when she was in her midforties. But her culinary education really began years earlier when, as a young bride, she began to teach herself how to cook. While she never undervalues what she learned in cooking school, most of the information that she has passed down to her children and grandchildren was learned from trial by fire. Here is some of my mother's kitchen wisdom, direct from the school of Adele, in her words . . .

* When baking a pie, to prevent the edge of the crust from overbrowning, place a strip of aluminum foil around the edge of the pie before putting it into the oven.

* Both biscuits and pie dough are very easy and simple to make from scratch. In order to keep the dough flaky, handle it as little as possible.

* Pie dough is one of the few foods that actually benefit from freezing. The freezing helps relax the gluten. Thus it may be convenient to make the pie dough ahead of time and freeze it for future use.

* Never add salt to a soup or sauce without tasting it first.

* Always store tomatoes with the stem-end down. They will last longer. And never put tomatoes in the refrigerator. Refrigerating tomatoes ruins their flavor.

* Do not store onions with apples or potatoes because the onions will make the apples and potatoes ripen faster.

* If you store potatoes in a crock, they won't turn green. Green potatoes are poisonous.

* To prevent the stinky green border around the yolk of a hard-cooked egg, put the egg (or eggs) in cold water and place on stove over heat. Bring to a boil and then immediately turn the heat down to a low simmer and cook for thirteen minutes. Then immediately take off heat and place eggs in cold water to stop the cooking process. The green border around the yolk is caused by a chemical in the white and a chemical in the yolk coming together under heat for too long. Remember, eggs are not soft- or hard-boiled. They are soft- or hard-cooked.

* When making a potato salad, use a firm potato such as Yukon Gold or White Rose instead of Idaho (which are mealy). The potato salad will stay tasty longer.

* When making fruit pies, add a tablespoon of fresh lemon juice. This will bring out the flavor of the fruit. Also, dot the filling with about a tablespoon of butter. This will enrich the flavor of the fruit. With stone fruits, such as peaches or cherries, a quarter of a teaspoon of almond extract enhances the flavor. Be careful though, as almond extract is very strong—less is more . . .

* When baking a cake, bake it at a lower temperature, such as 325 degrees Fahrenheit, for a longer period of time. The cake will rise more evenly and not have the hump in the middle. This is especially helpful when decorating a cake.

* Make your bread dough the day before (eighteen to twenty-four hours) you are going to bake. You will not have to use as much yeast, and your bread will have a better flavor.

* When hard water deposits have built up in a stainless-steel teapot, double broiler, or other stainless-steel pans, simmer unsweetened Kool-Aid in the pan, and the buildup will dissolve without scrubbing. (For those of you who own or work in a restaurant, the Kool-Aid works fantastic in cleaning steam tables. It will save hours and hours of scrubbing.)

* I always tell new cooks: "Just as all it takes to have a green thumb is brown knees—all it takes to be a good cook is a good recipe and the good sense to follow it."

# Chapter Seven

# WORK IT OUT

I wish that I had more to say on the topic. I wish that I could wax equally rhapsodic on the subject of reverse crunches as I can on *Pissaldiere* (savory Provençale *tarte* made with puff pastry and onions, preserved fish called *pissala*, or anchovies in a pinch, and olives). But I can't. I don't get excited about working out. I begrudgingly renew my gym membership, I drag myself there a few times a week, I work out, but never with the same enthusiasm that several of my friends do. I wish I had that chip in my brain that could thrill at the sight of an elliptical trainer. I wish my heart would race when I hear an aerobics instructor bark out steps in a room full of sweaty people. I have spent years trying to find that elusive endorphin high that runners supposedly get. All I've gotten are bad knees and an occasional stitch in the side.

So why do I include this chapter at all? Because exercise is a fact of life. We need to stay fit. Everyone should, though in my business it is a professional imperative. (Actually, in my business, I should be at least ten pounds *underweight*, if I really want to look like I'm in great shape, but I have to draw the line somewhere.) Some of us have metabolisms that just naturally burn calories, and we can eat whatever we want and have little to show for it in the way of jiggly upper arms and muffin tops. Others can run six miles every morning and then put on weight just walking past a Pinkberry. It hardly seems fair. I would say that I fall somewhere between these two categories. I inherited my paternal grandmother's tall yet curvy figure—the latter description being something that my grandmother tried her entire life to starve herself out of. She was an undiagnosed anorexic/bulimic who abhorred any sort of weight gain, on her or anyone else. I remember as a child listening to her boast that her waist could be measured by my grandfather putting his two hands around her waist, fingertips touching. I am pretty sure that food never held the same allure for her as it does for me. Food for her equaled shame—something to deny herself, or to immediately get rid of if she did indulge. Food for me equals a kind of wonder, a miraculous thing. You can create *that* with these simple ingredients? It's something that I would never want to give up, which means that I need to face the fact that the only way I can continue my love affair with food is to get in bed with the gym—and pretend I like it. Close my eyes and think of England . . .

The times when I have been the most successful at staying in shape have been motivated by love. Falling in love or falling out of love. The former being the easiest, since the endorphin kick from infatuation makes you feel like you can move skyscrapers—a few chaturangas are small potatoes. Yoga lends itself to this state very nicely. Falling out of love is usually more anger motivated, and every exercise can seem like a violent, almost vengeful act. It's a great time to take up boxing. But unfortunately, these two emotional states are short-lived and not dependable as fitness motivators. The desire to exercise needs to come from somewhere else.

My main motivator is to enable myself to enjoy life—eating what I want, drinking when I like, and preserving the status quo. I am not in the market to sculpt my body into some kind of armor, seeing how muscled and mannish I can become. I just want everything to basically stay in the vicinity of where it already is. Working out is a constant battle with gravity, and even though we know who wins eventually, it's still a battle that must be fought.

And if I stop being superficial for a moment (See? Fitness always brings out the superficial in me), there are other far more important reasons to get on a workout regimen and stay on one.

MOOD: Have you ever noticed how great you feel when you are steadily working out? As counterintuitive as it seems, regular exercise helps promote a higher energy level. There are days when I literally have to drag myself to the gym. I feel that I haven't got an ounce of energy to spare and all I can think about is how long I have to commit to working out before I can go home and crawl into bed. Then, miraculously, by the end of the hour I allotted myself, I find that I have twice the energy I came in with. This has happened more times than I can count, too often to be considered mere flukes.

Additionally, there is the overall mood enhancement that comes from seeing changes in your body after working out steadily for at least a month. You stand straighter. You look taller. Things don't poke out quite as much where they're not supposed to. It is a definite confidence booster and a great enhancement to your amorous life. Think about it: who wants to take off their clothes and bare their soul (let alone their backside) when they feel out of shape? Certainly not I.

FIGHTING OSTEOPOROSIS: Most of us think about osteoporosis in terms of our grandmothers or mothers. But the fact is that osteoporosis is highly preventable with exercise early in life. What we do in our twenties really does affect us in our forties and beyond. Steady exercise is the best way to build bone density, which can save you from falling down and breaking your bones later in life. And "later in life" comes much earlier than you think . . .

STRENGTH: Most everything we do in life is a little easier if we have strength. The best shape that I have ever been in was when I decided to singlehandedly install a roof garden in my fifth-floor walk-up in Manhattan (six floors, if you count the roof). Carrying fifty-pound bags of soil up six flights does incredible things to your shoulders. This

I would consider the best type of exercise, since it is sneaky exercise—meaning that you are getting fit without knowing it. My first priority was creating a beautiful garden, and everything else was just an added bonus.

There is a good feeling that comes with being strong. I don't mean a weird he-man, bodybuilding kind of strength (which doesn't seem like real strength to me at all, but rather a bizarre sort of body dysmorphia), but strength that allows me to accomplish things on my own without asking for help from anyone. And staying in shape allows me the kind of stamina that I need to chase my children around.

. . . . . . . . .

There are myriad other reasons to stay fit. (Look, I'm writing this as much for me as for you.) The question is, what to do? How to accomplish it? The way I see it, there are two different paths. The first, the most obvious, is the gym. You scope out all the nearby offerings—and the nearer the better, because as anyone who has ever belonged to a gym knows, if it takes more than ten minutes to get there, you might as well join a gym in Buenos Aires for all the time you're going to be spending there. Then once you find the place that has the right ratio of amenity to price for you—the swimming pool, the fresh towels, the cute guys (hey, whatever it takes!)—you sign up, work out for three weeks . . . and never go back.

Actually, that's not what has to happen. The gym route *can* work, but in my experience, for it to work for any real period of time, you need a way to make it consistent. That could mean signing up for lessons with a personal trainer—a great solution, but it can get pricey; finding

# YOGA VERSUS PILATES

For a lot of people, yoga and Pilates seem interchangeable.
I have to admit that for a while I was in that camp. My friend Brandi
teaches both yoga and Pilates, so I asked her professional opinion
about the differences between the two, in order to help people decide
what's right for them.

## YOGA

COST (GROUP LESSON):
$10 TO $20

COST (PRIVATE LESSON):
$50 TO $100

CONVENIENCE: Once you
learn Sun Salutation and a few
other poses, you can easily
practice yoga at home. (But
you'll miss the bare-chested
yogis doing warrior pose.)

BENEFITS: Amazing
flexibility, tone (without bulking up),
proportional strength, and increased balance. In addition, there is a
spiritual component to yoga that doesn't exist in Pilates. Yoga without
meditation is considered a shadow exercise, purely physical. The poses
are intended to prepare the mind (and soul) for meditation. Whether
you have spiritual leanings or not, odds are you'll feel more relaxed and
de-stressed after your practice.

**TIP:** At the risk of sounding unenlightened, I do believe that great yoga clothes can enhance your practice. Granted, it won't guarantee that you get your heels flat on the floor during Downward Dog, but you'll feel better knowing that you *look* better. My favorites are Lululemon and Christy Turlington's line Nuala.

## PILATES

COST (GROUP LESSON): $25 TO $35
COST (PRIVATE LESSON): $50 TO $100

**CONVENIENCE:** Like yoga, once you learn a basic Pilates mat routine, you can practice at home (usually with a video, to keep your pace consistent). However, proper technique is crucial to making strides, and so periodically taking private or group lessons to maintain your form is essential.

**BENEFITS:** With a huge focus on "core" muscles (abdominals, obliques, etc.), you'll quickly notice greater strength around your midsection. This will improve posture and balance—as well as performance in most athletic activities. Since Pilates requires both control and precision, it's ideal for perfectionists.

**TIP:** Pilates can definitely get pricey, given that most people prefer private sessions. There is a clever little work-around, however. For an aspiring instructor to become certified, she or he must first teach two hundred to five hundred lessons. Track down someone who is trying to reach this goal! Odds are good you can wrangle some free or heavily discounted lessons. At least until they're officially an instructor and no longer take your calls.

a gym buddy to motivate you and make sure you both don't just stay home and watch *American Idol* instead; or simply developing a set routine that you absolutely don't waver from. It should be as important as taking your children to school. Make it that important.

Whatever you do, be consistent and set yourself goals that you can achieve within a reasonable amount of time. There's nothing more discouraging than putting in serious time and effort, but failing to see the drastic results you expect. Make your goals realistic and attainable. It's better to accomplish three little things over a span of three months, and keep going, than to chase one big thing for six months and give up. I once became obsessed with developing that little muscle line under the shoulders (it's called the deltoid—the only muscle I can actually name). For six weeks I did lateral lifts and shoulder presses and all sorts of funky dumbbell exercises, and one day I looked in the mirror and there it was! The muscle—it popped! As excited as I was by the look of it, I was even more thrilled that I had stuck to it, that I had achieved my goal. I went home that afternoon and proceeded to parade around the house, flexing my muscles for my husband like a teenage boy. He wasn't as impressed as I was, I could tell . . . but maybe he was just jealous.

It also helps to remember where you came from. I'm guilty of this myself, especially when first going back to the gym after a long break (thank you, babies). We often forget just how far we've come. Rather than applauding our progress, we become focused on what we *haven't* accomplished yet. We ignore, or underappreciate, how our body is changing, and only notice what we're still dissatisfied with. Whether it's taking pictures or recording measurements or paying attention to clothes that once bound you like a seventeenth-century Han Chinese royal shoe and now you can breathe in, it helps to record your progress.

A second way to get in shape is to fall in love. No, not with a person, but with an activity. Rock climbing, salsa dancing, karate (or any martial art, for that matter), tennis, cycling, yoga, these are all great candidates for getting into shape without making a big deal about it. When you try a new sport or activity, or take up an old favorite again, you're practicing because you *enjoy* it—not because you want ripped abs. And as a consequence, you want to become better at it—to jump higher, to cycle faster, to dance more gracefully. Your motivation isn't superficial aesthetics, it's enjoyment. You want not only to experience it but also to make progress. Slowly, your body is transformed without your even noticing.

A close friend of mine, Sara, started training in tae kwon do when she was in her midtwenties. She grew to love it, reveling in the sensations of speed and power. I watched in amazement as, month by month, Sara's body transformed. She grew visibly stronger and more sinewy, she was vibrant, even her walk was different. I was about to sign up myself, I was so impressed by her results, when she abruptly informed me that she had dropped out and moved on to another less "full contact" sport. Apparently, being sinewy wasn't enough of a trade-off to getting kicked in the face. Hard. My husband, a third-degree black belt in tae kwon do, swears that it was an anomaly and to this day tries to get Sara to restart her training. He reminds her that she almost got her red belt. I remind her how amazing she looks in her wedding pictures. She takes the compliment but says she's sticking with Pilates, thank you very much.

A third, and somewhat unconventional, way to get in shape is through work. When I was starring in *Cabaret* on Broadway, I was dancing and performing eight times a week. Let me tell you, stomping around in the Weimar Republic while belting out "Mein Herr" is a *great* way to keep it off. Every night after the show, I felt both invigorated and exhausted. After the show, I ate like an Olympic champ—pretty much anything that didn't eat me first. And during the day, to ensure that I didn't injure myself while performing, I took up Pilates. The show was hard on my body; on top of the demanding singing and dance routines, I was running up and down circular staircases and changing out of costumes at breakneck speeds. And my dressing room was inexplicably located on the fifth floor, which didn't make things any easier. I used to bring my Pomeranian into work, and racing into the dressing room midperformance, out of breath, I'd spot her, happily asleep on the couch, and hate her just a little bit.

· · · · · · · ·

While getting in shape is a wonderful, inspiring, and at times life-changing thing to do, I feel that I need to address the fact that it can be taken too far. The point should always be to do something *good* for your body—to make your body the best and strongest that it can be. *Not* to exercise or diet yourself into starvation. It isn't news that there is a horribly unhealthy and ultimately unattainable body image that is plastered over every magazine. We all buy these magazines and read the articles about how we are supposed to feel good about ourselves, and at the same time we are treated to photos of a barely postpubescent model in a bikini that would be better suited to dental flossing. The double message is always there, and it can wreak havoc on the psyche. Even the healthiest of us are affected, regardless of our looks, professions, or ages. I was absolutely horrified when my five-year-old daughter asked her father and me, in all sincerity, if she was fat. (For the record, she isn't. In fact, I wish that I could keep a few more pounds on her, which isn't very easy, considering that I gave birth to the pickiest eater on the planet.) I calmly asked her where she got the idea into her head. Was it someone from school? Did she hear it on television? She shrugged and said "ballet." I cringed. My plan had always been to get her involved in ballet early, and then move her on to something else before all the crazy body-image stuff happens in the teen years. The last thing I want is to subject my own daughter to the kinds of life-threatening insecurities that so many dancers I have known have struggled with.

"It's just my tummy," Mathilda explained. "It sticks out."

"But, honey! It's *supposed* to stick out at your age. It's the way girl bodies are built! You would be unhealthy if it didn't!"

That night I started looking into tap lessons.

And as horrible as the models in the magazines can make us feel, there are the poor models themselves. One of my good friends was a former model as a teenager. She left school at sixteen and moved to Japan for work. Within the year she was hooked on diet pills (speed) and laxatives. She told me about all the times she would diet herself into a frenzy, only to have her booking agent take a Sharpie to one of her pictures and begin coloring in the outside of her already tiny thighs, telling her that she had to get rid of at least five pounds. And no matter how many five pounds she lost, there was always more to lose. It didn't take long for her to become anorexic. She flew back home to her parents in Ohio weighing eighty-eight pounds at five feet eight inches tall, and spent the next two years trying to learn how to eat again. Thankfully, Brandi is one of the lucky ones. She is now a successful fitness instructor, our children are best friends, and she is one of the healthiest and most beautiful women I know. When people ask us if we plan to get our children involved in modeling or acting, we both have the same shared sense of horror. Yeah, and why don't we just feed them to the lions while we're at it?

More than just about anything I want my daughters to grow up with healthy body images. I want them to be strong, so they can defend themselves on the playground. I want them to be fast, so they can outrun the boys. I want them to be fit, so they'll be around long after I am gone. I wish the same for all of us and our daughters. That's not too much to ask, is it?

# UNCONVENTIONAL WAYS TO STAY FIT

Every fitness magazine in the world will tell you to do things like "Take the stairs instead of the elevator" or "While waiting for the bus, do calf raises." Yeah, we know. But taking the stairs every day and freaking out fellow bus passengers gets old fast. So for those of you looking for some creative ways to stay fit, I asked my friend and personal trainer Steve Lake to estimate just how many calories can be burned by doing the following activities.*

### VIGOROUS AIR GUITAR

More calories are burned standing, obviously, and the heavier/faster the metal the better—average of 132 calories/hour, sitting; 197 calories/hour when standing.

### BENCH-PRESS YOUR BABY

You'll burn about 197 calories an hour doing this and develop some nice pectorals. Lying on your back, hand on each side of the baby body, press up and down—repeat 12 times. Rest and repeat for 3 sets. Make sure to make the baby giggle. Also make sure not to drop the baby. Um, that's even more important.

### REARRANGING THE FURNITURE

Depending on how aggressive you get about this, or how indecisive you are, you can actually burn off quite a bit. Provides a bare minimum of 165 calories/hour and the benefit of some strength training on top of all this—if you happen to favor Indonesian hardwoods.

*All calories burned are based on an average weight of 145 pounds and are per hour of activity.*

Additionally, here is a breakdown of some everyday activities that you'll probably be doing anyway. These aren't excuses to not hit the gym, but it's nice to know that while you're multitasking your life away, at least you're burning off that tiramisu.

* Dancing and singing to a Broadway musical album: 197 calories an hour (just singing by itself comes in at about 132 calories an hour)

* Digging in the garden: 329 calories an hour

* Pushing your baby (or someone else's) in a stroller: 164 calories an hour

* Baking: 164 calories an hour

* Loading and unloading the car: 197 calories an hour

* Chasing your kids around: 350 calories an hour

* Putting up a Christmas tree: 151 calories an hour

* Sweeping: 165 calories an hour

* Doing laundry/making the beds: 140 calories an hour of continuous folding and putting away

* Vacuuming: 165 calories an hour

* Kissing: 70 calories an hour
  (I hope this is an everyday activity. If it isn't, make it so . . .)

* Playing piano: 181 calories an hour

* Roller-skating: 460 calories an hour

* Reunion with family (sitting and talking—but not fighting): 99 calories an hour. Since the likelihood of any family reunion not involving fighting is astronomically slim, you should prob-ably tack on an additional 15 calories for the family squabbles.

# Chapter Eight

# OH, MAMA!

WE HAD JUST MOVED INTO OUR NEW HOUSE. I was in the kitchen, trying to find a place for the contents of the multitude of boxes I had needlessly shipped from New York. (Toothbrushes? Dishwashing detergent? Really?) My husband was writing on the porch, enjoying the California sunshine, while our daughter played in the garden. Suddenly I heard a gaggle of unfamiliar little voices that sounded as if they were just outside.

"Poop face! Butt head!"

And then my daughter's.

"Hi. My name is Mathilda. Would you like to meet my cat?"

"You are a penis, Vagina Head!" the voices replied, screeching in unison, followed by great howls of laughter.

"My cat's name is Pink Heart. You can pet her if you want," Mathilda offered, seemingly undaunted.

The insults continued. I put my boxes down and came outside to find five kids ranging from age three to six standing on the other side of our wooden fence calling my daughter every body part and function their little minds could make up. It was a dizzyingly assorted array of anatomical combinations. Interestingly, "penis" seemed to be the most regular standby, while "vagina," though more rare, seemed to carry much more weight, garnering the greatest admiration from the crowd (as measured in eruptive titters). I briefly wondered about the sociological implication of this but figured it probably just came down to the most number of syllables.

"It seems Mathilda is being introduced to the neighborhood," my husband remarked. He seemed as undaunted as Mathilda.

"Have you told them to stop?" I asked. "They shouldn't say things like that."

"Of course I did," he said. "Obviously to great effect."

I marched to the fence and faced down the unruly crowd.

"Hello, there. I'm Molly and this is Mathilda. What are your names?"

"Penis, butt, poop, poopface, vagina head!"

This was going to be tough. I persevered.

"Hey, look guys," I said—and truth be told, they were mostly boys, with the exception of one little sister, who spent most of the time sucking her thumb, releasing it for the occasional giggle. "Mathilda, her daddy, and I just moved into the neighborhood, and I'm sure that Mathilda would love to play with you, but we need to stop with the name-calling!"

"We don't have to do anything you tell us. You aren't our mommy!" one little boy said, puffing out his chest defiantly.

Unbeknownst to the tiny hoodlums, I had already met their parents at a neighborhood cocktail party a few days before.

I crouched down to their level and looked them right in the eye.

"I know each and every one of your parents, and if you don't stop the name-calling right now, I'm going to find your mommies and tell them what you've been saying."

Mathilda watched the showdown wide-eyed. There was a dramatic pause, then one little boy whooped and hollered, letting loose a Lilliputian yet surprisingly savage war cry, "PENIS POOP PEE PEE JERK MUD FACE VAGINA NOSE!"

Good God. I move into the most laid-back, beachiest community possible and yet somehow manage to enter *Lord of the Flies.*

I lunged for the gate, and the kids went scrambling, scattering in all directions like pigeons.

"Take it easy!" my husband called after me. "They're kids!"

I marched down to the neighborhood hangout where many of the parents liked to congregate and chat. One boy ran as fast as his five-year-old legs could carry him as I stalked behind him like the grand executioner. He reached his mother a few seconds before me and sputtered out his story as quickly as he could.

"A bunch of us . . . but I wasn't . . . I mean, I did, but not the bad stuff . . . It was Henry. I didn't . . ."

His mother looked at me questioningly and tried to calm her apoplectic son. I smiled and attempted to explain the situation, which in the retelling seemed significantly less grave. She nodded at me.

"Yes, Miro is experimenting with his language skills."

"Right. Well he seemed to have a pretty good grasp on what he was saying."

We laughed. She nodded. I nodded. We both stood there, nodding

at each other until I realized that she had no intention of reprimanding her kid. Instead, she gently suggested that her son go into the house and calm down for a minute, and when he reappeared she bent down on one knee and proceeded to question him about *how he felt.* It was a self-help parenting book in action. *Wait a minute,* I thought. *Are we seriously talking about his feelings? What about my daughter who was called names for the last ten minutes?* Meanwhile, another mother wearing a baby in a sling (the mother of Henry, the worst offender) corralled her son to stand before me. I stood and waited for her to explain to her son the error of his ways.

"OK, Henry," she said to her son. "This lady has something she wants to say to you."

I gulped. I didn't want to say anything to her son. What I wanted was an apology. What I wanted was some form of parenting that resembled my own in some small way. Were these kids being raised to become politicians? Learning never to apologize at the risk of appearing wrong? Henry looked up at me with an expression like, "Come on, lady. I got other people to harass." I improvised something along the lines of how he was welcome to come over and play, but that we have rules about name-calling, etc. He looked at me blankly. "So, that's it," I concluded. "Thanks for talking to me, Henry."

"OK?" the mother said, adjusting the baby sling. "Are we good?"

When I got home, my husband was doing dishes in the kitchen. He smiled at me.

"You're such a badass!"

· · · · · · · · ·

We all have models of what we consider to be good parenting. If we're lucky, we have a positive personal example from which to model our own unique brand of parenting. Both my husband and I were lucky; we have good relationships with our parents and, for the most part, very fond childhood memories. I feel that my parents set the bar pretty high. My mother never let a holiday or birthday pass without doing something incredibly crafty and creative. Homemade decorated gingerbread cookies. Hand-sewn Halloween costumes. Decorated doll cakes on our birthdays. She never failed to deliver.

Even so, there are ways that we choose to do things differently from our parents. A lot of it is based on the fact that times change. My parents were products of the fifties—postwar, pretherapy. Children were expected to speak when spoken to. My parents broke away from their upbringing drastically to raise us, but there was still a level of one-sided communication and unquestioning obedience that seems out of touch in today's world of psychological nuance. Communication and reflection are undeniably important. As annoyed as I was by Miro's parents' obsession with their child "communicating his feelings," I was only annoyed that it so clearly superseded—even ignored—thinking about someone else's feelings. But I do think it's important that children learn to express their feelings, to understand how and why they feel the way they do about things. Sometimes, though, it can go too far and veer into self-obsession. This is the tricky part of promoting intensive self-awareness. We all know someone who's been in therapy for years, who is tuned into their every slightest motivation, impulse, and emotion, and yet who at the same time remains painfully oblivious (or uninterested in) how other people are feeling. Raising a child who is emotionally aware, yet not destined to become an egotist, takes finesse, persistence, and frankly, a bit of luck.

The other problem with the belief that every problem can be solved if you just allow your child to communicate his or her feelings—what I call Talky-Feely Parenting—is that it overlooks that you're dealing with a *child*. While I'm often amazed at my daughter Mathilda's command of logic and her fresh perspective on everything, the fact remains that she is five years old; there are certain things she can't communicate, nor should she be able to. I don't even think it's healthy to try to engage in that kind of communication 24/7 with our children. I don't like it as an adult! Do you remember how annoying it is when someone is trying to find out how you feel all the time, even before you yourself have had a chance to feel it? "Why aren't you smiling? Are you in a bad mood? What's going on?" Why would I want to subject my own child to this emotional cross-examination?

# THINGS NOT TO FEEL GUILTY ABOUT WHEN YOU HAVE A CHILD

**THE HOUSE WILL BE A MESS.** Not only will it be messy almost all the time, but it will also be full of the ugliest purple and green and striped pink plastic contraptions ever designed by childless toymakers. Instinctively, it seems your child will only play with something if he or she knows you are embarrassed to own it.

**YOU'LL GET MAD AT YOUR PARENTS.** Whether your parents are the type who mysteriously lose all ability to care for a child as soon as yours appears, or whether they suddenly manifest a heretofore nonexistent obsession to play with kids, you can be sure that somehow they will still manage to annoy you. Get over it. Save your therapy dollars for diapers.

**YOUR KID DOESN'T PLAY THE PIANO, JUGGLE, SPEAK MANDARIN CHINESE, AND SWIM COMPETITIVELY.** While this phenomenon is most apparent in the cities, the suburbs are certainly no strangers to the one-upmanship that parents engage in. It's OK if you think Baby Einstein is unbelievably irritating. It is irritating. Einstein never watched Baby Einstein—and he did all right.

**YOUR KID IS A PICKY EATER.** At times it feels as if our eldest daughter exists on air and Pirate's Booty—which is just cheese-dusted, packaged air (ohhh, but it's organic!). Yet she is tall and healthy and has enough energy to wear down two adults every day. So why then do I feel like a bad parent? Because on her first day of kindergarten, as the children were volunteering their favorite food during circle time, half of them offered up "sushi." One especially hard-core kid specified and chirped, "Seaweed!" My husband and I felt ourselves sinking deeper into our seats. Just as we were about to slink out of the room, branded as the world's worst parents, a little girl proudly declared her favorite food was "Sugar!" Guess who's coming over for a playdate?

**YOU SPEND TIME WITH YOUR SIGNIFICANT OTHER.** This one should be completely obvious, although it's strikingly difficult to implement. The flip side of having kids that really like you is that it becomes nearly impossible to carve out time to spend with your significant other. As hard as it is to explain to your child why Mommy and Daddy need special time with each other, it is absolutely imperative to the health of your primary relationship. I believe it's better for your kids in the long run to have parents who still want time with each other than ones who see the other as a mere coparental custodian. There are only so many episodes of *Blue's Clues* that you can endure together before it's time to banish your adorable tyrant, order in Chinese, and spend time with your "better half" doing what you do best . . .

Assuming that everything can be resolved solely through communication is a somewhat utopian idea of child rearing. It discounts so many other elements. Desire. Impulse. Conflict. Too much chocolate milk. There is nothing that I find more maddening than being somewhere with my child and waiting while a Talky-Feely Parent enacts an impromptu therapy session and makes their child go through a litany of "feelings" to explain away bad behavior. Sometimes the kid gets so into it; I watch them squeeze out a tear as they eye the toy that is just out of reach, knowing that they just need to provide the right buzzwords and they'll get it back. I feel like yelling, "You're being suckered! How can you not know that?!"

Not to say that my children are perfect, or that I am the perfect parent. There was a long week when my daughter Mathilda's response to any question was "Liar liar pants on fire." This was a vast improvement upon the previously and often used "Nana Nana, butt butt." I don't ask her why she says these things; I know she's picked them up at school. She's just trying them on for size, and eventually she will find the words for what she feels. I trust that. We are all works in progress. And believe me, I'm no expert when it comes to being a mother. I just like to say that my expertise lies in the fact that I *am* a mother and incidentally, I play one on TV . . .

· · · · · · · ·

It's hard being a parent. There are so many conflicting models out there, all of them with their pros and cons. The Crunchy Parents, whose child has never eaten anything that isn't sprouting. The Luddite Parents, who won't allow their child to watch a movie—ever—because their child

could get "overstimulated." The Let-It-Ride Parents, who give their children complete and utter free rein. The Never-Too-Young-to-Learn Parents (my husband often falls into this category: he started teaching Mathilda about gravity when she was two years old, using soap bubbles to demonstrate; by the age of four she was a staunch advocate of evolution, announcing to everyone she met, "I believe in apes!") and their nemeses, the Don't-Ask-Me Parents.

The variety and degree of difference among parenting styles can be overwhelming; it extends to every facet of child rearing. There's no better example than breast-feeding, an issue that seems to inspire judgment and disagreement wherever it rears its head. I try to be as open-minded as possible, but I have to admit that it's still difficult for me to understand the appeal of breast-feeding children until they're in elementary school. It's a personal choice, though, and I respect it accordingly. To be fair, it's one of the most personal choices you can make. I chose to breast-feed for as long as I possibly could, and then pumped so enthusiastically that I had an additional three-month supply waiting in our freezer like some kind of Ben & Jerry's for babies. This was mostly due to my husband, whose Mussolini-like fascination for order and scheduling extended to the breast pump. My breasts were pretty sure that they were out for hire—and feeding a royal army. The weekend I attempted to wean "naturally" turned me into a sorry sight. For two days, I lay on the couch, sipping sage tea with two cabbage leaves pressed to each breast. I looked like I was wearing a bikini in *Land of the Lost*. On Monday, I broke down and went to the doctor and had him prescribe me some medication. My husband swung by the pharmacy on his way home from work to pick up the prescription.

"These better make you really high or something," he said, handing me the bottle. The pills cost $280 and weren't covered by insurance.

"Why did you buy them?" I asked. "That's crazy!"

"Well, you looked like you were in so much pain."

Honestly, I was. I took the pills and started to feel normal within twenty-four hours. When I saw my doctor a couple of days later and asked why the pills were so expensive, he seemed shocked. It was only after looking up the medication online that he found out that they are also prescribed as a new and better form of Viagra.

I am grateful that my body was able to nourish my child, that she was able to get all of the antibodies needed to bolster her own immunity. I think La Leche League is a wonderful organization, and I'm happy that they have gone a long way to abolish the bizarre stigma that was still quite prevalent when my mother was raising her babies. But color me old-fashioned, I personally feel that it is a good idea to put the kibosh on breast-feeding when your kid can clearly verbalize a preference for left or right.

. . . . . . . .

And then there are our own parents. It doesn't matter how old you are, there is something about having your own parent watching *you* parent that always feels like you're at an audition. Did they like the way I tested the formula on the back of my hand? Did they approve of how I took "colorful rainbow kitty-cat" off the table until she finished her pasta? What about how I let it pass when she told me I was a "mean mommy" because I wouldn't let her go down to the swing set until she put her toys away? I find myself having to remind myself that *I already have the job!*

This is, of course, in my own mind. My parents don't necessarily judge us on our child rearing, or if they do, they are polite enough to keep it to themselves. Once in a while, though, they can't help but let it slip. "She's playing you," my dad will grumble. There are certain things they can't understand about the choices that we make.

At the moment, our family has to commute back and forth between Los Angeles, where I work on a television show, and Palo Alto, where my husband attends Stanford Business School. Mathilda takes it badly each and every time her father leaves Sunday night. I know how heartbroken she feels; I feel the same way. Every Sunday and Monday are the same. She cries and says "I miss Daddy" nonstop, as a mantra. My own father was visiting on one of these weekends, and I tried to explain to him that it was a hard adjustment for her. My father's response was, "Well, she's just got to deal with it."

"What do you mean, 'she just has to deal with it'? She *is* dealing with it. She just misses him."

"Well, sure. But she has to deal with it. That's life."

I found myself prickly with anger. How can he be so unfair? Why am I made to feel like a sucker because I know that it is the healthy thing to let her cry and express how much she misses her father, instead of imposing the "stiff upper lip" maxim that I grew up with (to some extent, my father to a greater extent). It occurred to me that my father's father worked on the railroad and must have been gone for long stretches at a time. How did he feel about it? Then there was the time when my own family was separated for close to a year while we made the move from Sacramento to Los Angeles. Change is hard for anyone, but especially for children who have no real frame of reference for time.

A day can seem like a month, a month can seem like a year. I remember that, and I feel for my daughter. I let her know that it's OK with me if she wants to talk about how she feels. OK, I confess. Sometimes, I am one of those Talky-Feely Parents too.

Then there are my husband's parents. They were Greek immigrants who raised their children in Massachusetts and moved back to Greece as soon as my husband entered college. Our daughter Mathilda is the first granddaughter in the family, and the second we arrive in the country, the grandparents, aunts, and uncles greet us at the airport armed with gifts. And Papou (as her Greek grandfather is called) makes sure that there is more where that came from.

"They're spending too much money," I whisper to my husband.

"Let them. They want to."

These are not wealthy people. They are hardworking former immigrants who put their children in the very best prep schools in Massachusetts by owning a pizzeria. And yet every time they see Mathilda, it is Christmas *and* Easter *and* the Fourth of July. They look for every excuse to spoil her, and they do.

Since we live in the United States, we try to spend one month a year in Greece so they can spend time with their firstborn granddaughter. Having not lived with my parents since I moved out of the house at eighteen, I lightly asked my husband, the first time we made the trip to Greece, if we should be staying in a hotel near the house.

"Sure, if you want to mortally offend them," came the reply.

We stayed in the house. And thus began my big fat Greek life.

Mothering around your mother is one thing; mothering around your mother-in-law is another. What do you say when your mother-in-law says or does something that is completely different from the way that you like to do things? When it's my own mother, I basically just snap at her and act like an obnoxious teenager. "Don't tell me what to do. I'm a grown-up." I'm surly and immature. Defensive and overly sensitive. But my parents know me. They know that there is a pure beating heart underneath all of the fear, and having lived with me through my teen years, still loving me, I never worry. I know they love me beyond measure, and at the end of the day, nothing else really matters. When it's your mother-in-law . . . it's a little trickier. It's nice if you are loved by your in-laws, but there is still no familial obligation. They are basically taking their son's word for it—that I'm worth it. But in truth, it takes years to really get to know someone. Factor in another language, and this learning curve can get even steeper. Even more than the difference in language, however, is the difference in culture. I fell in love with a man in New York City, who was raised in Massachusetts. Then we got serious, and I flew halfway around the world to meet his Greek family, where everything is different.

My daughter even has a different name when we are in Greece.

. . . . . . . .

At some point in our courtship, my husband (then boyfriend) told me about the Greek custom of naming the firstborn child after the father's parents. Names stay in the family for generations. Cousins all share the same names. It all seems a bit confusing and strange to someone of my Anglo-Saxon background. (The closest we have is the Jr./Sr. title, but girls aren't often named after family members, at least not as an obligation.) When I became pregnant and found out it was a girl, there came the sinking realization that I was expected to name her after my mother-in-law. Not to say that I don't love my mother-in-law, I do. She is a magnificent woman, smart as a whip, hardworking, a phenomenal cook, and full of love for her family. And she raised the person I chose to love, which alone is enough for me. But my whole life I dreamed about having a child and naming that child. I started collecting possible name combinations when *I* was still a child; how could I just give all that up and name my child based on a tradition from a culture in which I wasn't even raised?

I informed my husband that I had a problem with the name thing, and he was silent. I presented my reasons for my refusal. He listened, but I could tell that it was going to be a problem.

"What's the matter?" I asked, knowing the answer.

"I just don't know how to tell my mom. It's just so . . . disrespectful," he said. "It's like a slap in the face."

"It isn't fair," I wailed to my mother.

"It's just a name," my mother said

"Just a name? How can you say that? *You* named all of your kids. I didn't see you naming any of us after Grandma Aloha." I actually had a Grandma Aloha—my father's mother. She wasn't Hawaiian, nor did she live in Hawaii. Apparently *her* mother listened to some radio station while she was pregnant and liked the sound of the word *aloha*. Another daughter was christened Coral. (Strangely, my other grandmother lived in Hawaii. But her name was Edith.)

"Well, it's different," my mother reminded me. "It isn't a part of our culture. It didn't matter to your father, or his family. Not like it does to yours."

# PARENTING **ADVICE TO IGNORE** (EVEN IF IT'S FROM YOUR OWN MOM)

Our friends recently got pregnant and, upon showing up for dinner, explained that they were exhausted. "How can you be exhausted *before* having kids?" I asked. They explained, that they had just come from a six-hour new parent seminar. Yes, you read that right, six hours. Sure, parenting can be tough at times, but you don't need six hours to learn how to change their diapers and make them hate you when they're teenagers. In my experience as a new parent, I was inundated with advice, some of it welcome, some of it . . . not so much. Following is the advice I'm glad I ignored.

To spare the feelings of friends and family, I've refrained from naming the contributors (you too, Mom).

## WORST ADVICE

* Let them "cry it out."

* Don't let your baby cry—ever.

* If you hold a newborn too much, you'll spoil him.

* Don't ever let them suck their thumb—it'll ruin their teeth.

* Assume all behavior is diet related (Grumpy? Give 'em soy! Hyperactive? Take away gluten!).

I pouted. "But *I'm* not Greek!"

"No, but you love one," she reminded me.

"Why don't you compromise?" my mother suggested. "Give her the Greek name as a middle name."

So it was decided. We named her Mathilda Ereni. But for one month out of the year, her name is just Ereni.

It was presented to the in-laws as a choice to give our child an American name *and* a Greek name. When they lived in the States, everyone in their family had an Americanized version of their Greek name. Stylianos became Steve, Irini became Irene, and so on; consequently, this compromise was accepted with little fanfare. Her American name would be Mathilda, and her Greek name Ereni. But somewhere in the back of my mind, there was that little bit of expectation. (You know what I'm talking about. It's like meeting a guy who loves football and thinking, *Well, when he really falls in love with me, he'll decide that going to the theater is so much more interesting . . .*) After a while, I reasoned, they would just accept that her name is really Mathilda. That's the name she answers to. And look at her! She is *clearly* a Mathilda.

But guess what? My in-laws refuse to call her anything but "Ereni." Ereni or the diminutive "Erenoula" (the Greek version of "Little Irene"). There is a reason why the Acropolis is still standing. Greek culture was built to last.

I unwrapped her christening gifts and found diamond-studded "Ereni" necklaces. Bibs, Onesies, *everything* emblazoned with *Ereni*. For this one month out of the year, it felt somehow like my daughter was taken away from me. I know this is ridiculous, but it felt to me that this should be one of the inalienable rites of motherhood. The right to name your own child, and to have everyone else in the world acknowledge your choice. Your children grow up and make their own decisions about their identity soon enough. Is it so wrong to want to guard that right when you have it? "Don't be selfish," the mature voice would scold me. "Get over it." And then the other voice: "This might be the only child you ever have! How can you be such a doormat? If you can't even stand up for her name, how are you going to stand up to anything for her?"

I finally lost it one night as my husband and I were driving around a Greek beach town, looking for an Internet phone card. (The remote location still hasn't heard of WiFi.) I dissolved into tears and screamed out my frustration and feelings at being steamrolled by the culture.

"Why do they insist on calling her by a name that isn't hers? Can't they see? Can't they understand that it's important to me?"

"No," he said. "I don't think that they understand how important it is to you. I don't think that *I* understood how important it was to you. I thought that we . . ." He trailed off, at a loss.

We drove around in silence, and then cruised by the outdoor movie theater to see what was playing. (Incidentally, you haven't lived until you have experienced *Mamma Mia!* with a bunch of chain-smoking Greek Abba fans.)

On the way home, my husband was the first to speak.

"I'll talk to my mom. I'll tell her that she has to be called Mathilda."

A wave of relief passed over me. I felt like a mosquito bite that was just agonizing me suddenly vanished. And then, concern.

"But wait! What will you say? She'll know it's me!"

"No, I promise. I won't make it sound like you. I wouldn't do that. I'll say it's for Mathilda . . . that it's confusing for her. Don't worry."

He smiled at me, and in that smile I remembered all of the reasons why I married the guy. This is a man who is very close to his mom but who would still stand up for me. The best of both worlds.

"OK," I said. "Thanks. I want to . . . give me the night to think about it. Do me a favor and just let me think about it some more."

Just knowing that he would take my side, that he would hear me out and not tell me that I was wrong, or neurotic, or unfair, made my feelings . . . not change exactly, but it did feel like the pressure cooker that had become my head just lost some of its steam.

The next day we all left the house for our afternoon beach romp. Mathilda and I splashed around in the children's tide pool and tried to catch little fish with leftover pita and a sand pail, but had much more success with the sand crabs. She showed off her impressive bucket of sand crabs to a little posse of Greek girls.

"Tell them my name, Mommy."

"You tell them," I told her "Don't be shy."

Mathilda looked at them and cocked her head to one side shyly.

"Ereni," she said. With a perfect Greek accent.

And then she chased the girls shrieking into the water with her bucket full of sand crabs.

At that moment I realized the obvious. I wasn't taking anything away from my daughter by letting her have this other identity for one month out of the year. She was receiving the gift of another culture and the love of a few very important people from that culture. Our children benefit not only from all of the love that we give them but also from all the love that they get from everyone else in the world—the more the better. I feel like I'm the best mother that I can be when I allow other people to love my daughter in their way. It's not always easy. But I'm learning all the time what it means to be a mother.

A while later I sat next to my mother-in-law at a dinner party in Athens. Friends of the host were making polite conversation with us (in English, since I have a long way to go until I have perfected my Greek). They inquired about my daughter, her granddaughter, and then the inevitable question, "What's her name?" I turned to my mother-in-law and, unbelievably, heard her start to say "Mathil—"

Could my husband have said something, or did she just intuit something from me?

"Ereni," I interrupted. "Her name is Ereni. She's named for her Yia Yia."

The look on my mother-in-law's face is one that I won't soon forget. Relief. Gratitude. Pride. Love.

In the same week, I managed to feel like a good mother and daughter. Sometimes, I realized, it's the same thing.

· · · · · · · · ·

As parents we are always looking for the right thing to do. When I was pregnant, my husband and I had lengthy conversations imagining every possible situation and how we would handle it. We thought we had a pretty good handle on it and felt hopeful and confident about embarking upon our new roles as parents. I remember being in the ICU when Mathilda was a baby. She was born early, at thirty-five weeks, and as a result spent a week in the hospital while they monitored her "bilirubin" level. Having never even heard of bilirubin (a brownish yellow substance found in bile, produced when the liver breaks down old red blood cells; since premature babies don't have livers functioning at full capacity yet, too much bilirubin can cause jaundice—as well as brain damage, hearing loss, and all sorts of other undesirable things), my husband and I trekked back and forth to the hospital in the snow, bemoaning bilirubin. We started referring to him as "Billy" and then "Billy the ICU bully."

One night we were sitting in the Neonatal ICU, holding her. It was three o'clock in the morning. The room was dark save for the warm blue glow emanating from the other incubators. We stared at her tiny face in wonder and cooed at her. How much we loved her, how perfect she was. A nurse turned and said, "Just wait till she's thirteen years old and she won't speak to you because you won't let her wear a pair of jeans that say *Bootylicious* on the seat." We looked at each other in shock and then laughed. Would we be that parent? Impossible! Not us. Not *our* little angel.

Five years later, I am surprised at the ways she has found to test me. She isn't even a teenager yet! I have actually found myself negotiating, and when that didn't work, literally begging my daughter to wear a pair of overpriced patent leather boots I bought for her. Other times I have resorted to the desperate invention of an "Imaginary Girl" who will give hugs and kisses when my own daughter withholds. This, by the way, works like magic. It basically creates a dynamic of sibling rivalry when there are no siblings. (You don't love me? Well, Imaginary Girl thinks I'm *swell* . . .) My husband, though initially amused, suggested that it might not be the healthiest impulse to foster in our child, and I had to agree with him. Soon I decided to faze her out, explaining to my daughter that Imaginary Girl was gone.

"Where did she go?" Mathilda asked me.

I hadn't thought about that.

"Um, she went back to *her* imaginary home . . . to her imaginary mommy and daddy."

"Oh," Mathilda said. Then after a moment, "Does she have an imaginary cat?" Mathilda has an obsession with cats. Before Imaginary Girl was retired, Mathilda was careful to make sure that Imaginary Girl wasn't somehow one-upping her, and scoring a pet before she did.

"No. Imaginary Girl is waiting to get a cat, just like you are."

"Oh," Mathilda said. "Then that's OK."

There was a few months' reprieve from Imaginary Girl. I felt incredibly sheepish about my invention, and for a while whenever I expressed a parental opinion to my husband I got an eyebrow raise and the two words. *Imaginary Girl.* Fair enough.

Then one day, to our surprise, Mathilda brought her back for a return engagement.

"One whole inch longer than Imaginary Girl," Mathilda remarked as she brushed her own hair.

"I wouldn't know," I told her. "Imaginary Girl left, remember?"

"Yeah, but she came back," she insisted.

"I don't know about that . . ."

My reluctance caused Mathilda to put down the hairbrush. With an exasperated sigh, she turned to face me.

"She's *pretend*, Mommy. You *know* that, right?"

She does have a remarkable grasp of what is real and what isn't. It made me realize that I wasn't getting away with anything. She knew all along. She just enjoyed the play of it. It tickled her funny bone.

It has since been determined that Mathilda rides her bike better, swims faster, and sings prettier than Imaginary Girl. She is smarter, can eat more peas, and says thank you more often. In fact, it has been generally decided that Mathilda is all around better in every way than poor little Imaginary Girl. When I'm asked whom I love more, her or the Imaginary Girl, I tell her that I love her and just how much. And then I sing, "Ain't nothing like the real thing, baby . . ."

# BEST MOM
# MOMENTS

I asked my friends to remember the best things their mothers ever did for them. As surprising as the range of experiences was, equally surprising were the power and vividness of these memories. Reading this, it's a tribute to all mothers and makes you realize that everything you do as a mother counts, and will be remembered.

**ILANA (ACTRESS):** To turn over a new leaf. Whenever we got into conflict, we would sit down after we talked it through and take a leaf and turn it over, which was the symbol of starting over, with a new beginning, and learning from what just happened.

**JULIA (COSTUME DESIGNER):** Made sure my brothers and I had a delicious meal together every night. I can't think of a meal growing up that was not cooked with love.

**SANDY (ACTRESS):** My mom told me never to wear mauve or olive green. They're not my colors.

**SARAH (MUSIC INDUSTRY EXEC):** She told me right before she died (I was in my early twenties) that the best thing she did was raise kids who were going to have a great and happy life together, even knowing how desperately they'd miss her and even if she couldn't be there to share it day by day.

**MARISA (EDITOR):** Told me repeatedly that life isn't fair.

**JAMES (ARCHITECT, WRITER):** My mother was a remarkable woman, an urbane and sophisticated New Yorker with, among other things, a strong and distinctive fashion sense. When she would appear for my elementary school parent-teacher conferences in, say, a poncho outfit with matching wool muffler—a superbly stylish mid-sixties look—it drove me crazy. "Why can't you look like the other mothers?" I'd complain. She would express some concern, but then proceed to go on her way, following her instincts about clothing as well as many things . . . a confident and fearless attitude that, years later, I realized was perhaps her greatest gift to me.

**ELIZABETH (STUDENT):** She taught me the importance and beauty of giving people room to be who they are. That, and how to hand-fold a towel, back-comb my hair, moonwalk like Michael Jackson, and lead a mean campfire song.

**PANIO (WRITER):** When I was four, my mother let me walk to preschool by myself every morning. Strutting along the sidewalk of our tiny town of Shelburne Falls, passing storefronts while swinging my red Snoopy lunch box, I felt unbelievably proud and grown-up. It was a stunning counterpoint to preschool where, speaking almost no English, I would hide by the aquarium. After I became a father and began taking my daughter to preschool, I called up my mother and asked, "Are you completely crazy? You let me walk to school by myself! I was four years old!" "Of course I didn't let you," she told me. "I kept about twenty feet behind you—close enough to make sure you were safe, but far enough so that you didn't know I was there and would feel like a big kid."

**TODD (WRITER):** She always made me feel like I'd get a second chance if I made a mistake.

**COLIN (DANCER, ACTOR, SINGER):** The embrace of my mom. My favorite place to this day is probably in the arms of my mother.

Chapter Nine

# WHAT DID YOU WANT TO BE WHEN YOU GREW UP?

IT'S ALL TOO EASY TO LOSE SIGHT OF WHAT'S IMPOR-TANT TO US. Life seems particularly skilled at throwing distractions, obstacles, and outright roadblocks in our path. One of the hardest parts of dealing with the inevitable complexities of managing to pursue what inspires and fulfills us is that much of the time we get in our own way. I realize I'm veering dangerously into self-help book territory here, and I want to explicitly refrain from anything like that. I don't know how you should live your life and wouldn't presume to tell you. All I know is that based on my experiences, and the experiences of my friends and family, what seems to be a recurring theme is the importance of staying true to ourselves. Once you start living your life entirely for someone or something else—whether it's familial, social, or professional respon-sibilities wholly motivating you—then you find yourself in a life that doesn't seem to belong to you. Before you get to an existential crisis that feels like you've been plunked down in a Talking Heads song—"*And you may ask yourself / Where does that highway go?*"—stop and look at where you are and whether it's where you want to be. How far away are you from the original dreams you had when you were younger? Did you give up those dreams because you changed your mind, or did you give up because life pulled you away and you couldn't find your way back?

When I was a little girl, I wanted to sing. More precisely, I wanted to be a jazz singer. When I was in second grade, we were given an assignment to study the life of a famous American and to present their life story as that person. Unlike my fellow classmates, who chose the more common American heroes and heroines—George Washington, Florence Nightingale, and Dolley Madison—I chose the great jazz singer Bessie Smith. When American Life Story day rolled around, I showed up to present my chosen famous American dressed in a twenties-style dress, high heels, and with my father in tow, accompanying me on the piano as I told stories to the class about the Empress of Jazz's life and sang a couple of her biggest hits, including the unlikely elementary school crowd pleaser "Gimme a Pigfoot and a Bottle of Beer." (Miss Kestenbaum was a very progressive second-grade teacher.) Happily, my report was highly entertaining for the other kids, and I was thrilled at how it turned out. I was doing what felt right—singing, acting, and writing.

As I got older and began acting in films, I lost sight of the other two activities. For some odd reason, I didn't feel that you could do more than one thing. I don't know where I got this idea from, but I just stopped singing altogether. Same with the writing. And as much as I love acting, I know that it isn't all that I do. Acting is my chosen career,

it is my livelihood, which gives it a kind of pressure that my other talents don't have. It took years but I finally got it through to myself that I can sing if I want. A little while back, I put together a jazz group with a few talented guys, and we perform gigs when I can. No publicity, very little money, no expectations; just the joy of singing the music I love.

I know I'm not the only person to have experienced this sort of epiphany. Time and again I've spoken to people or known friends who have stopped and looked at what they were doing in their lives and realized that it was not the life they had envisioned for themselves. Sometimes it involves a drastic step—leaving a career, going back to school, even ending a relationship that is deeply unsatisfying. But more often, it's the little steps that matter; carving out a little time for yourself to pursue something you really love.

My friend Sara is a successful director of publicity for a major publishing house. She is extremely good at her job, but there was always something that seemed to be missing. She started taking classes in shoe making at FIT. Sara has always been a great shoe aficionado (with immaculate taste), so why not learn how to make them? Twice a week, after work, she went to her class at FIT and learned the artisanal skill. A few years after that, she moved on to making jewelry, a skill at which she is extremely gifted. (I try to steer my husband in her direction around Valentine's Day and anniversaries.) Maybe one day she thinks she will pursue it as a full-time career, but for now it is just enough to remind her that her job is not all she does, it isn't all she is.

As we get older we have a lifetime to look back on, to observe the different interests associated with the different stages. I'm sure there is a lot that you would love to forget (That goth phase? The nineties grunge? That boyfriend no one liked—for good reason), but there is just as much worth remembering. The time you stayed up all night with a friend who just broke up with her boyfriend, the fearlessness you felt backpacking through Europe. The openness of your heart the first time you fell in love. Take the good and figure out how to incorporate it into your life and leave the rest where it belongs—in the past.

In the future, it's up to us to decide who we want to be, how we want to live the second act (or third, depending on how we define the different periods of our life). The way I see it, there's the first act, infancy (we didn't have a whole lot to say). The second act (we have *too* much to say). And then there's the third act, where we realize there's a lot we don't know, but thankfully there's also a lot we do. It's the act of restraint and of the calculated risk. Hopefully we have enough wisdom to know that we don't need to prove anything anymore, and enough life history to know when we need to try new things, to be the navigator of our own unforgettable journey.

# ACKNOWLEDGMENTS

The temptation here is to thank everyone that I've ever known since they have all played a part in providing me with the experiences and inspiration that went into writing this book. So a big global thank-you. That means you.

More specifically, I would like to thank everyone at HarperCollins, particularly Brittany Hamblin for her insightful editorial suggestions, and my copy editor, Shelly Perron, who very kindly forgave my sentence fragments, and my design dream team, Robin Bilardello for the beautiful cover, and Lorie Pagnozzi for the inspired interiors. A special thanks to Carrie Kania for her incredible enthusiasm, and for sharing my vision of the book and making sure that it happened. Even with unforeseen events and all the attendant delays, your support and graciousness never wavered, and I am proud to be one of the It imprint's flagship books.

Thank you to all of my friends who so generously contributed their humor, advice, and expertise: Mike Albo, Todd Thomas, Dr. David Colbert, Taite Pearson, Brandi Sanger, Steve Lake, Marie Viljoen, and Justin Bond (for the funniest sidebar that I could not include—rest assured, it's going in the director's cut).

And also to my dear friends, many who allowed me to include their personal stories, tribulations, and triumphs, and to many more who offered opinions on music, makeup, mothers, wine, cheese, and any of the other various subjects I expounded upon: Victoria Leacock Hoffman, Dr. Jennifer Ozeir, Darcy Cosper, Sara Nichols, Meredith Arthur, Matt Freeman, Dr. Greg Henderson, Will Ryman, Julia Caston, Alex Auder, Kenny Mellman, Jason Weinberg, Greg Clark, David Daley, Colin Dickerman, James Sanders, Ingrid Bernstein, Jessica Leigh Brown, Marisa Bowe, Ilana Levine, Chris Pavone, Todd Simmons, Elizabeth Burdick, Sarah Harden, Sandy Fleischer, Wendy Waddell, Thomas Weems, Hill Solomon, Colin Cunliffe, Julian Fleisher, Kenny Cummings, Deborah Treisman, Stephanie Pearson, Peter Smith, Amy Sparks, Erin Guth, Molly Ryan, Valerie Baugh, Carl Stanley, Valentina Tiurbini, Cindy Sherman, and David Byrne.

My beloved teacher Irene Brafstein. I miss you.

I would also like to thank:

Mary Oliver, whose magnificent poetry I found myself reading often during the course of writing this book, and whose craftsmanship and graceful mastery alternately astonished, consoled, and inspired me. The poems recalled the sensation of immersing my hands in the loamy earth of my garden—which is to say, of being connected to something greater than myself. You always remind me of how much the right word matters, an invaluable gift to any writer.

Michael Pollan, for making so much sense.

John Cheever, not only for reminding us of the "salvation of prose" but for inadvertently and fortuitously leading me to my husband through the elegance of *his* prose. I am deeply grateful to the Cheever family for allowing me to include their father's glorious writing in my book.

Ruben and Isabel Toledo—I remember meeting both of you all those years ago. Elegant Isabel with all of those vintage keys around your neck; Ruben with your inimitable style and moxie. Thank you for illustrating my book and bringing it to life. Having your involvement was a dream come true.

My dear friend Fergus Greer, for helping me find the pretty when I needed to most.

Barbara Foley, for holding the hope.

My family—I know it hasn't always been easy to be related to me and everything that goes with the whole "celebrity" thing. Thank you for your understanding, love, and shelter.

Beth Ringwald Carnes and Dr. Kenneth Carnes.

Chance Podrasky, Lillie and Jenna Carnes.

Kelly Ringwald and Eileen Descallar Ringwald.

Naomi Burns, you deserve a medal.

Irini and Stylianos Gianopoulos, Katerina, Makis, and Aphrodite Tatsos: thank you for welcoming me into your Greek family.

Robert and Adele Ringwald—the most extraordinary people I know. How blessed I am to have you as parents. This book is in many ways a Valentine to you, Mom, but it's also about you, Dad, because you were the man who had the good fortune and foresight to find her and to hang on to her. Mom, you taught me to be a woman I am proud to be. Dad, you taught me how to sing. Thank you for that and for teaching me to hear the music in everything.

There are certain very important people who were instrumental in helping me get to the finish line during that last month. You will never know how much your intelligence, love, and compassion kept me afloat during this time. You are my chosen family and I value you beyond words. Victoria, Matt, Greg, Brandi, and Meredith—how lucky I am to have you in my life.

Susan Raihofer, every writer should be so lucky to have an agent like you. Your passion and attention to detail are unparalleled—not to mention your patience! Thank you for believing in me and telling me that my book would arrive at the right time. Who would have thought that the idea for this book would have come from lunch in that awful restaurant in the West Village? I look forward to many more lunches and just as many books together.

Thank you, Adele and Roman, for so patiently waiting for me to finish this book before making your wondrous presence known to the world. I can't wait to get to know you better!

And Mathilda, there is no better muse that a mommy could ask for. You are forever a surprise, a delight, and a bottomless fount of inspiration. Your advice on life is more succinct than anything I could ever write, so as a postscript I will include it here: "None of this matters. All that matters is that you stay alive and that you like your life." Thank you, my lovely girl.

Finally, I would like to thank the one person without whom this book would never have been written—my husband, Panio Gianopoulos. Your contribution is immeasurable. From putting me on a writing schedule (two hours or five hundred words, whichever comes first) to making me trust my written voice when my confidence faltered. You are my first and finest editor and greatest champion. It is deeply daunting now writing this without your discerning eye and kind judgment. I thank you for making room for two writers in the family (and based on early evidence from Mathilda, I would wager that we'll have three, if not more, heaven help us . . .). Most of all, I thank you for helping me learn what it means to love another person completely. To understand, to forgive, and to transcend. To soar and to fall from our invincible heights—toward each other and in love.

*S'agapo.*